Law of Medical Negligence for Medical Professionals

Dr Navin Kumar Gupta

Ukiyoto Publishing

All global publishing rights are held by

Ukiyoto Publishing

Published in 2023

Content Copyright ©Dr Navin Kumar Gupta

ISBN 9789360498665

www.ukiyoto.com

Contents

Introduction

The number of cases of alleged Medical Negligence against medical professionals, nursing homes and hospitals in various consumer commissions and a few in criminal courts are increasing and several decisions are being passed against them.

Every doctor, nursing home and hospital must have a basic understanding of what constitutes Medical Negligence so that they can keep themselves well within the framework of the law.

When doctors treat patients, various factors determine the line of treatment, the medicines to be given and the aftercare. There may be different lines of treatment available and different medicines that could be possibly given. The doctor has to make a considered decision. And the decision may not be the only one, or the perfect one.

Sometimes despite doing everything possible, a patient dies or suffers some permanent infirmity. He, or his relatives, drag the doctor, nursing home or hospital to litigation for Medical Negligence. A few lawyers assure them of extracting heavy compensation.

At the same time, doctors do commit mistakes inadvertently and the suffering patient is certainly entitled to damages. This is the reason why every doctor, nursing home and hospital should have Indemnity Insurance. The insurance company will bear the financial burden. And the premiums are nominal.

This small treatise explains the principles of Medical Negligence in simple words and the consequential liability both for the doctor, nursing home and hospital as well as the patient. We have also added the text of the following important Acts for ready reference:

1. National Medical Commission Act, 2019

2. Clinical Establishments (Registration and Regulation) Act, 2010

3. Maharashtra Nursing Homes Registration Act 1949 (All states have their own Nursing Home Regulations)

If anyone has any query or issue relating to Medical Negligence, he can contact Dr. Binoy Gupta through email: (eleena100@ hotmail.com) for totally free consultation.

This is an additional free service we are offering to our readers.

Dr. Navin Kumar Gupta
Dr. Binoy Gupta

Medical Negligence

Meaning of Medical Negligence

In simple language, Negligence is the breach of a duty caused by omission to do something which a reasonable man would do or doing something which a prudent and reasonable man would not do.

I am dealing only with Medical Negligence for which some legal action can be taken by a patient against a Doctor, nursing home

or hospital. Medical Negligence involves the following 3 elements:

1. There must be a legal duty to exercise due care;

2. There must be a breach of the duty; and

3. This should have resulted in consequential damages.

So far as persons engaged in the Medical Profession are concerned, it may be stated that every person who enters into the profession undertakes to bring to the exercise of it, a reasonable degree of care and skill. A doctor or a surgeon does not undertake that he will positively cure a patient nor does he undertake to use the highest possible degree of skills as there may be persons more learned and skilled than him, but he undertakes to use a fair, reasonable and competent degree of skill.

This implied undertaking constitutes the real test of what is Medical Negligence. This has been laid down in the judgment in Bolam vs. Friern Hospital Management Committee (1957) 2 All ER 118(a UK case), in which McNair, J., summed up the law as under:

"The test is the standard of the ordinary skilled man exercising and professing to have that special skill. A man need not possess the highest expert skill; it is well-established law that it is sufficient if he exercises the ordinary skill of an ordinary competent man exercising that particular art. In the case of a medical man, negligence means failure to act in accordance with the standards of reasonably competent medical men at the time. There may be one or more perfectly proper standards, and if he conforms with one of these proper standards, then he is not negligent."

Poonam Verma vs Ashwin Patel & Ors (SC) decided on 10 May 1996

(This test first formulated by a UK court is commonly known as the Bolam Test and is followed by the Supreme Court as well as all courts and consumer commissions in India.)

Qualified Doctor and Registered Hospital or Nursing Home

The first important and most obvious requisite to avoid any litigation is that the Doctor treating a patient should be qualified in the particular field or speciality.

Section 34(1) of the National Medical Commission Act 2019 (which has replaced the Indian Medical Council of Act 1933) stipulates that:

a) No person who is not enrolled in the State Register or the National Register of the Medical Council can practice medicine as a qualified medical practitioner;

Hold office as a physician or surgeon or any other office, by whatever name called, which is meant to be held by a physician or surgeon;

Sign or authenticate a medical or fitness certificate or any other certificate required by any law to be signed or authenticated by a duly qualified medical practitioner;

Give evidence at any inquest or in any court of law as an expert under section 45 of the Indian Evidence Act, 1872 on any matter relating to medicine: and their obligations thereto.

Section 34 (2) states that any person who contravenes any of the provisions of this section shall be punished with imprisonment for a term which may extend to one year, or with fine which may extend to five lakh rupees or with both.

A general practitioner is not qualified to do surgery. An eye surgeon is not qualified to do ear surgery. An Ayurveda practitioner cannot prescribe Allopathic medicine. A Homeopathy doctor is not allowed to practice Allopathy. The Hospital or Nursing Home where the treatment is taken must be duly registered under the State Registration law (if applicable). It should have the requisite number of qualified staff, necessary equipment and must maintain the prescribed registers.

It follows that a doctor can practice medicine only in the system in which he is qualified. But it is common practice in Maharashtra and Gujarat and some other places for Homeopathy or Ayurveda doctors to practice Allopathy medicine, prescribe Allopathy medicines, give Allopathy injections and even do some minor surgeries.

Due to the acute shortage of Allopathy doctors in Primary Health Centres and remote areas, for the past several years, there have been suggestions to introduce a 1-year bridge course after completing which BAMS, BHMS, etc. doctors will be able to prescribe Allopathy medicines. These persons will be known as 'mid-level practitioners'. They will be able to prescribe Allopathy medicines at the Primary Health Centres or at remote Centres.

The Govt. of India has introduced the concept of Community Health Provider in Section 32(1) in the National Medical Commission Act 2019 which contains provisions to grant limited licenses to practice medicine at mid-level as Community Health Provider to such persons connected with a modern scientific medical profession who qualify such criteria as may be specified by the regulations. The Regulations will be framed in due course. The Govt. of India is trying to introduce the 1 -year bridge course. This matter has been challenged and is pending in different courts.

Case Study - Homeopathy doctor practicing Allopathy

Dr. Ashwin Patel, a Homeopathy doctor in Anand, Gujarat, examined Pramod Verma who was suffering from fever at Pramod Verma's residence on 4 July 1992. Dr. Ashwin Patel was practicing Allopathy medicine and kept Pramod Verma on Allopathy drugs for viral fever up to 6 July 1992; and thereafter, for typhoid fever. The condition of Pramod Verma deteriorated. On 12 July 1992, on the advice of Dr. Ashwin Patel, he was shifted to Sanjeevani Maternity and General Nursing as an indoor patient. Pramod Verma received treatment there till the evening of 14 July 1992 when he was transferred to the Hinduja Hospital in an unconscious stage. Within four and a half hours of admission in Hinduja Hospital, Pramod Verma died. His wife filed a Consumer Complaint alleging negligence and claiming compensation. The matter went up to the Supreme Court.

The Supreme Court held that a person who does not have knowledge of a particular system of medicine, but practices in that system is a quack. Such a person is guilty of negligence per se. No further proof is needed.

Poonam Verma vs Ashwin Patel & Ors (SC) decided on 10 May 1996

What constitutes Medical Negligence

The standard of skill required from a doctor is that of an ordinary man in that profession. There may be more than one option. If he chooses any of those, then he is not negligent. Neither the very highest nor a very low degree of care and competence judged in the light of the particular circumstances of each case is what the law requires.

"The test is the standard of the ordinary skilled man exercising and professing to have that special skill. A man need not possess the highest expert skill. It is well established law that it is sufficient if he exercises the ordinary skill of an ordinary competent man exercising that particular art. In the case of a medical man, negligence means failure to act in accordance with the standards of reasonably competent medical men at the time. There may be one or more perfectly proper standards, and if he confirms with one of these proper standards, then he is not negligent."

Bolam V. Friern Hospital Management Committee (1957) 2 All ER 118. McNair, J. summed up the law relating to Medical Negligence.

Note: This is a decision of the UK. But commonly termed as the Bolam Test for Medical Negligence, it is followed by all courts in India.

Duties that a Doctor owes to his patient

A doctor owes certain duties to his patient. A breach of these duties constitutes Medical Negligence. These duties have been specified by the Supreme Court.

"The duties which a doctor owes to his patient are clear. A person who holds himself out ready to give medical advice and treatment impliedly undertakes that he is possessed of skill and knowledge for the purpose. Such a person when consulted by a patient owes him certain duties, viz., a duty of care in deciding whether to undertake the case, a duty of care in deciding what treatment to give or a duty of care in the administration of that treatment. A breach of any of those duties gives a right of action for negligence to, the patient.

The practitioner must bring to his task a reasonable degree of skill and knowledge and must exercise a reasonable degree of care. Neither the very highest nor a very low degree of care and competence judged in the light of the particular circumstances of each case is what the law requires.

The doctor no doubt has discretion in choosing treatment which he proposes to give to the patient and such discretion is relatively ampler in cases of emergency."

Laxman Balkrishna Joshi vs Trimbak Bapu Godbole And Anr (SC) decided on 2 May 1968

Vicarious liability of Hospital

The aggrieved persons normally file complaints against the doctor(s) as well as the concerned Nursing Home or Hospital because it is far easier to recover larger compensation from a Nursing Home or Hospital. The Supreme Court has held as follows:

"It is well established that a hospital is vicariously liable for the acts of negligence committed by the doctors engaged or empanelled to provide medical care. It is common experience that when a patient goes to a hospital, he/she goes there on account of the reputation of the hospital, and with the hope that due and proper care will be taken by the hospital authorities. If the hospital fails to discharge their duties through their doctors, being employed on job basis or employed on contract basis, it is the hospital which has to justify the acts of commission or omission on behalf of their doctors."

Maharaja Agrasen Hospital & Ors Versus Master Rishabh Sharma & Ors. (SC) decided on 16 December 2019.

Doctors' Duties & Patient's Consent

In India, Indian Medical Council (Professional Conduct, Etiquette and Ethics) Regulations, 2002 contained the law relating to medical negligence and informed consent. These regulations have been replaced by the "National Medical Commission Registered Medical Practitioner (Professional Conduct) Regulations, 2023" with effect from 2nd August 2023.

I am listing some of the important Regulations. Anyone wanting the full regulations can write to me on my email.

Chapter 1

Professional Conduct of RMPs (Registered Medical Practitioners)

3. Suffix and Modern Medicine:

(A) Every self-employed RMP shall display his/her registration ID in his/her prescription, certificate, and money receipts given to patients. Employed RMP shall get a seal made by the employer displaying the unique registration number below the RMP's signatures. Note: RMPs must give their Registration number in all prescriptions, certificates, receipts, etc.

(Guideline for prescription)

(B) The RMP shall display as suffix to his/her name only NMC recognized and accredited medical degrees/diplomas as provided in the nomenclature of the regulations and listed on the NMC website (List of such Degrees and Diplomas will be on the website and updated regularly). RMPs qualified abroad and seeking registration to practice after clearing MGE/NEXT must use NMC-approved equivalent Medical prefixes and suffixes to provide clarity to patients and the public at large. (L1).

Note: RMPs can suffix to their names only degrees and diplomas recognized by the NMC.

(C) RMP shall not claim to be a clinical specialist unless he/she has NMC recognized training and qualification in that specific branch of modern medicine (The list of recognized post-graduation and super-specialization degrees/diplomas will be available on the NMC website) (L1 and/or L2)

Note: Specialists can practice only in the particular branch of their specialization.

(D) Every RMP shall practice the system of medicine in which he/she has trained and certified (for this purpose referred to as modern medicine* or allopathic medicine) and shall not associate professionally with any unqualified person to perform any treatment, procedure, or operation. (L2)

(E) RMP shall not employ in connection with his/her professional practice any healthcare professional who is neither registered nor trained under the relevant Medical Acts in force related to the practice of modern medicine. Provided that having employed any such assistants in the practice, the ultimate responsibility rests on the self-employed RMP or the RMP responsible for administration and recruitment in case of hospital practice.(L2).

*"Modern medicine" or "Allopathy" is a healthcare discipline that involves a scientific understanding of disease processes and uses rational and evidence-based treatment methods. This system of medicine views disease as a biological abnormality in the function or structure of organs or organ systems, with effects on organs and the body as a whole. Animal experiments may be used to understand disease processes and the efficacy of therapeutic measures. Medical research using blinded studies and statistical analyses informs all aspects of diagnosis, testing, treatment, and disease prevention. Modern medicine has international uniformity in theory and practice.

It has found universal acceptance in India and is currently practiced and taught in Government and Private hospitals and medical colleges governed/regulated and accredited by the National Medical Commission, Government of India.

Note: RMPs should not allow non- Allopathic doctors to perform procedures and surgeries.

4. Continuing Professional Development Program (CPD):

A RMP should attend continuing professional development programs regularly each year, totaling at least 30 credit hours every five years. Only recognized medical colleges and health institutions or medical Societies accredited or authorized by EMRB/State Medical Councils can offer trainings and credit hours for this purpose. Credit hours awarded shall be updated online against the Unique Registration Number of RMP on the EMRB-NMC website. Renewal of License to practice should be done every 5 years (from the publication of the Gazette notification), after submitting documentation of CPD credit hours. The license renewal form will allow updates of details like specialization, place of work, address, contact details, or any other detail specified by EMRB/NMC.(CPD guidelines)(L2).

Note: This makes CPD training of 30 credit hours every five years compulsory.

5. RMPs will be licensed to practice in the states after payment of requisite fee in States and their names will appear on state medical register.(L2)

6. Right to remuneration of RMP:

Consultation fees should be made known to the patient before examination or treatment of the patient. A reasonable estimation of the cost of surgery or treatment should be provided to the patient to enable an informed decision. RMP can refuse to treat or to continue to treat a patient if the fees, as indicated, are not paid. At the same time this does not apply to doctors in government service or emergencies but the doctor must ensure that the patient is not abandoned. (L1)

Note: RMP should give an estimate of his fees and cost to the patient before examination or treatment to enable him to make an informed decision.

7. Prohibiting Soliciting of Patients:

RMP shall not solicit patients directly or indirectly or as a part of the group of RMPs, or institutions or organizations or hospitals or nursing homes, or corporate hospitals established, owned, controlled, or maintained by the appropriate government, local authority, trust, whether private or public, corporation, co-operative society, organization or any other entity or person. (L2)

Note: RMPs should not solicit patients.

8. Prescribing Generic Medicines:

Every RMP should prescribe drugs using generic names written legibly and prescribe drugs rationally, avoiding unnecessary medications and irrational fixed-dose combination tablets. (L1 and/or L2) (Generic Drugs and Prescription guidelines)

9. Prohibition of Fee Splitting/Commissions:

A RMP shall not directly or indirectly participate in any act of division, transfer, assignment, subordination, rebating, splitting, or refunding of any fee for diagnostic, scanning, medical, surgical, or other treatment. These provisions shall apply with equal force to the referring, recommending, or procuring by a RMP of any patient, specimen, or material for diagnostic purposes or other studies/work. However, nothing in this section shall prohibit payment of salaries by a qualified RMP to another duly qualified person rendering medical care under his/her supervision. RMP shall not use online forums or agents for procuring patients. (L3).

10. Prohibition of endorsement of a product or person:

A. RMP individually or as part of an organization /association/society etc. shall not give to any person or to any companies or to any products or to software/platforms, whether for compensation or otherwise, any approval, recommendation, endorsement, certificate, report, or statement concerning any drug brand, medicine, nostrum remedy, surgical, or therapeutic article, apparatus or appliance or any commercial product or article with respect of any property, quality or use thereof or any test, demonstration or trial thereof, for use in connection with his name, signature, or photograph in any form or manner of advertising through any mode nor shall he boast of cases, operations, cures or remedies or permit the publication of report thereof through any mode. (L3)

B. A RMP shall not issue certificates of proficiency in modern medicine to unqualified, unskilled, or non-medical persons. This does not restrict the proper training and instruction of bonafide students, midwives, dispensers, surgical attendants, or skilled mechanical and technical assistants & therapy assistants under the personal supervision of RMPs. (L2). Every certificate must contain the details regarding experience, skills and competency obtained, duration of the training, and kind of work done during training. The onus of the veracity of the certificates lies with the RMP. (L2)

11. Advertisement:

A. RMP is permitted to make a formal announcement in any media (print, electronic or social) within 3 months regarding the following: (1) On starting practice (2) On change of type of practice (3) On changing address (4) On temporary absence from duty (5) On resumption of practice (6) On succeeding to another practice (7) Public declaration of charges. (L2).

Note: RMPs cannot advertise themselves except in the above exceptional cases.

B. RMP or any other person including corporate hospitals, running a maternity home, nursing home, private hospital, rehabilitation center, or any type of medical training institution, etc. may place announcements in the print, electronic and social media, but these should not contain anything more than the name of the institution, type of patients treated or admitted, kind of doctors and staff training and other facilities offered and the fees. (Guidelines on social media conduct) (L1 and/or L2)

C. RMP is allowed to do public education through media without soliciting patients for himself or the institution (L2)

12. Responsibility of RMP regarding the sale of drugs:

A. RMP shall not run an open shop to sell medicines prescribed by RMPs other than himself or for the sale of medical or surgical appliances. They are allowed to sell medication only to his/ her own patients. (L2)

B. RMP can prescribe or supply drugs, remedies, or appliances as long as there is no exploitation of the patients. Drugs prescribed by RMP or bought from the pharmacy for a patient should explicitly state the generic name of the drug. (L2)

C. RMP shall not administer, dispense or prescribe secret remedial agents of which he does not know the composition or action in the body. The manufacture or promotion or use of these remedies is prohibited. (L3)

Note: RMPs cannot open medicine shops and cannot prescribe secret remedial agents.

13. Responsibility of RMP regarding the Medical Records:

A. Every self-employed RMP shall maintain medical records of patients (inpatients) for 3 years from the date of the last contact with the patient for treatment, in a standard proforma laid down by the NMC. (Guideline) (L2)

B. If any request is made for medical records to RMP responsible for patient records in a hospital or healthcare institution either by the patient / authorized attendant or legal authority involved, the same may be duly acknowledged and documents shall be supplied within 5 working days. (L2)

C. In case of medical emergencies, efforts should be made to make the medical records available at the earliest. (L2)

D. Efforts shall be made to computerize patient's medical records for quick retrieval and security. Within 3 years from the date of publication of these Regulations, the RMP shall ensure fully digitized records, abiding by the provisions of the IT Act, data protection and privacy laws, or any other applicable laws, rules, and regulations notified from time to time for protecting the privacy of the patient. (L1, L2)

E. RMPs are in certain cases bound by law to give or may from time to time be called upon to give certificates, notifications, reports, and other documents of similar character, signed by them in their professional capacity for subsequent use in the courts or administrative or other purposes. Such reports, certificates, or documents should not be untrue, misleading, or improper. A self-employed RMP shall maintain a Register giving full details of such certificates issued by him/her. (L3)

Note: This Regulation is very important and prescribes the records RMPs must maintain and how to supply copies when asked for.

14. RMP shall cooperate in the investigation against incompetent, corrupt, unethical or dishonest conduct of other members of the profession without fear or favour. (L1)

15. The RMP shall not aid or abet torture, nor shall he be a party to either infliction of mental or physical trauma or concealment of torture inflicted by another person or agency in clear violation of human rights. (L3)

16. Practicing active euthanasia shall constitute unethical conduct. However, in some cases, the question of withdrawing life-supporting devices or measures even after brain death shall be decided following the provisions of the Transplantation of Human Organ Act, 1994 and follow prevailing law regarding the issue. (End of Life Guidelines)

17. The RMP should respect the boundaries of the doctor-patient relationship and not exploit the patient for personal, social, and business reasons (L2) and in particular, avoid sexual boundary violations. (L4)

18. RMP shall not refuse on religious grounds alone to assist in or conduct of sterility, birth control, circumcision, and medical termination of pregnancy when there is a medical indication. (L3)

Professional Misconduct:

Chapter 5 of the Regulations contains a list of acts which constitute Professional Misconduct

37. Professional Misconduct:

ny violation of these Regulations, or other applicable Acts related to medical practice which are in force, shall constitute professional misconduct. By issuing these Regulations, the EMRB, NMC, and the State Medical Councils are in no way precluded from considering and dealing with any other form of professional misconduct by registered medical practitioners which do not fall under any of the categories mentioned in the regulations or guidelines or codes appended. RMPs bound by these Regulations will not engage in any activities which violate these regulations and should not enter any employment or other contract that engages in activities in violation of any of these regulations. Conviction of RMP in cases of a cognizable offence involving moral turpitude may result in the suspension of license to practice.

Note: Professional Misconduct has been given a very wide definition. EMRB, NMC, and the State Medical Councils can consider and deal with any other form of Professional Misconduct which is not included in the definitions.

38. Procedure for a complaint of professional misconduct:

A. The aggrieved person will file the complaint to the State Medical council through the website portal/offline, ordinarily within 2 years from the cause of action. (The complaint will be lodged in the SMC where RMP is located at the time of cause of action, both in teleconsultation or in person consultation)

B. Where the aggrieved person is unable to make a complaint on account of physical or mental incapacity, a complaint may be filed by —

a a family member or relative or friend; or

b the guardian or authority under whose care treatment was received; or

c the legal heir or guardian in case of death of the patient; or

d The NMC/EMRB/State Medical Council can initiate a suo-moto case against any RMP taking cognizance of gross misconduct. The suo-moto complaint will be taken up if a simple majority of the NMC/EMRB/State Medical Council members agree to proceed against the RMP.

Note: This regulation deals with the Procedure for filing complaint of Professional Misconduct. Who can file it and where. Normally the aggrieved person will file the Complaint. NMC/EMRB/State Medical Council can also take up complaints suo moto (on their own).

39. Manner of Inquiry into the complaint:

(A) At the time of filing the complaint, the complainant shall submit to the EMRB or State Medical Council five copies for offline applications (till the whole process is made online) of the complaint along with supporting documents and the names and addresses of the witnesses.

(B) On receipt of the complaint, the SMC/EMRB/NMC shall send one of the copies received to the respondent within 15 working days. For online complaints, the State Medical Council/EMRB/NMC will send an e-copy and/or physical copy of the complaint to the respondent.

(C) The respondent shall file his reply to the complaint along with his list of documents, and names and addresses of witnesses, within a period not exceeding 15 working days from the date of receipt of the documented complaint.

(D) The state medical council or EMRB/NMC shall conduct an inquiry into the complaint following the principles of natural justice.

(E) On receipt of the complaint, the State Medical Council shall refer the case for review to the designated committee, with assistance from a panel of experts, if required, specifically formed for this purpose in the stipulated time.

(F) The /State Medical Councilor EMRB/NMC shall have the right to terminate the inquiry proceedings or to give an ex-parte decision on the complaint if the complainant or respondent fails, without sufficient cause, to present herself or himself for two consecutive hearings or three hearings in total convened by the /SMC or EMRB/NMC. In such situations, the termination or ex-parte order may not be passed without giving a notice of fifteen days in advance to the party concerned.

(G) The parties shall not be allowed to bring in any lawyer to represent them in their case at any stage of the proceedings before the state medical council or EMRB/NMC.

(H) In conducting the inquiry, a quorum shall be ensured.

(I). No new documents or certificates or evidence or witness will be entertained from either of the parties once the proceedings are initiated (meaning -after the parties have been called for a hearing) unless its admission is cleared by the majority of the members. The complaint cannot be withdrawn after it is admitted by the SMC or EMRB/NMC.

(J). The State Medical Council or EMRB/NMC may either of its motion or on an application made by either of the parties have the power to change the subject matter experts, if appointed, by providing a valid reason.

Note: This regulation deals with the Procedure to be followed by State Medical Council or EMRB/NMC after filing of complaint of Professional Misconduct. No party can bring any Advocate.

40. Disposal of the Complaints:

The State Medical Council or EMRB/NMC after giving the parties concerned an opportunity of being heard, may make any of the following recommendations:

1) Dismiss the complaint

2) Censure/Warn/Reprimand the RMP

3) Recommend counseling to the RMP

4) An alternative penalty can be considered

(Guidelines for alternative penalties can be given by EMRB as and when required)

5) May restrain the RMP from performing the clinical procedure(s) or examination as deemed fit. Holding Suspension i.e. restraining RMP from practice until the case is decided- only with full consensus (Restrain will only be in subject matter of dispute).

6) Suspend the RMP from practice for a temporary period as it may deem fit by removing the name of the RMP temporarily from the National Medical Register.

7) Award monetary penalty as it deems fit as per Section 30 of the NMC Act, 2019 can be given by SMC/EMRB only as and when required and will go to SMC/EMRB/NMC account.

8) SMC/EMRB/NMC can charge monetary penalty upto 10 times of the license fee in case it is found during misconduct complaint case that the RMP has not taken license to practice in the state. (L1 and/or L2).

9) May direct the RMP to undertake specific training courses related to the misconduct/some certificate course/ethics sensitization etc.

10) Permanent removal from NMR under exceptional circumstances by SMC must be ratified by EMRB.

11) Any suspension of RMP will automatically restore at completion of suspension period.

Note: This regulation deals with the Disposal of the Complaints - what orders the SMC/EMRB/NMC can pass.

41. Prohibition of review of the order:

SMC or EMRB/NMC will not have the power to review its order, and the order will be executed only after the expiry of the period of appeal.

42. Power of the SMC/EMRBNMC:

The SMC and EMRB/NMC shall have the same powers as are vested in a civil court under the Code of Civil Procedure, 1908 while trying a complaint against an RMP in respect of the following matters, namely:
1) The summoning and enforcing the attendance of any defendant or witness and examining the witness on oath.

2) Requiring the discovery and production of any document or other material object as evidence.

3) Receiving evidence on affidavits.

4) The requisitioning of the report of the concerned analysis or test from the appropriate laboratory or any other

5) Issuing of commissions for the examination of any witness, or document; and any other matter which may be prescribed by the Central Government.

6) Penalty (L2 to L5) so awarded and confirmed to the RMP by State Medical Council or EMRB/NMC shall be publicized widely on its website and other platforms as they deem fit and communicated to the employer, the hospital/healthcare institution of the RMP and respective Medical Associations/Societies/Bodies.

Note: This regulation gives the SMC and EMRB/NMC the same powers as vested in a civil court under the Code of Civil Procedure, 1908 in respect of the matters mentioned above.

43. Delay in decision:

Where the EMRB is informed that a complaint against a RMP has not been decided by a State Medical Council within six months from the date of the complaint, and the EMRB has reason to believe that there is no justified reason for not deciding the complaint within the said prescribed period, then EMRB can direct the SMC to hear the case on day to day basis until the case is duly heard and is closed or may withdraw/transfer the complaint pending with the concerned State Medical Council immediately. The reasons for not deciding the case within the stipulated time shall be mentioned in the order of the SMC. Registrar of the council or person mandated for such job by SMC act will be responsible for making all communications in time to everyone. *Note: Under this regulation, the State Medical Council has to dispose off the Complaint within 6 months. In case of delay, the EMRB can intervene.*

44. Appeal:

1) RMP who is aggrieved by the decision of the State Medical Council shall have the right to file an appeal to the Ethics and Medical Registration Board (EMRB) within 60 days from the date of receipt of the order passed by the said State Medical Council: Provided that the Ethics and Medical Registration Board may if it is satisfied that the appellant was prevented by sufficient cause from presenting the appeal within the aforesaid period of 60 days, allow it to be presented within a further period of 60 days.

2) RMP who is aggrieved by the decision of the Ethics and Medical Registration Board may prefer an appeal before the National Medical Commission within 60 days from the date of passing of an order by the EMRB.

3) Order of SMC will become operational after the expiry of the period of appeal (60days+60days). Once in appeal, the order of SMC will be deemed stayed unless decided otherwise by EMRB/NMC. *Note: This regulation prescribes the manner in which an RMP can file appeal against the order passed by the State Medical Council.*

Informed Consent:

It is the duty of the medical practitioner to obtain the informed consent of the patient before conducting any medical procedure or treatment. In several instances, the patient is made to sign on a blank form. This is unethical and illegal.

Informed consent means that the patient should be fully informed about the nature, purpose, and consequences of the treatment or procedure, and has voluntarily agreed to undergo the same.

The medical practitioner must ensure that the patient has understood the information provided and is capable of making an informed decision. In cases where the patient is not able to give consent, the medical practitioner must obtain the consent of the next of kin or legal guardian.

If a medical practitioner fails to obtain informed consent, or if the patient's consent was obtained by misrepresentation or fraud, it could amount to medical negligence. The patient may have a right to compensation for any harm or injury suffered as a result of such negligence.

The Supreme Court of India has rendered several decisions on the issue of informed consent and medical negligence. Some of the notable cases are:

In *R.K. Dalmia v. Justice S.R. Tendolkar (1959)*, the Supreme Court held that a medical practitioner must obtain the informed consent of the patient before conducting any medical procedure or treatment, and the consent must be based on full and fair disclosure of all material facts. The Supreme Court held that the patient has the right to be fully informed about the nature, purpose, and consequences of the treatment or procedure, and that the medical practitioner must ensure that the patient has understood the information provided and is capable of making an informed decision.

In *P. Rathinam v. Union of India (1994)*, the Supreme Court held that the principle of informed consent is a fundamental right of the patient and that a patient has the right to refuse treatment. The Supreme Court held that a medical practitioner must obtain the informed consent of the patient before conducting any medical procedure or treatment, and that the consent must be voluntary and without any duress or coercion.

In *Javed v. State of Haryana (2003)*, the Supreme Court held that it is the duty of the medical practitioner to obtain the informed consent of the patient before conducting any medical procedure or treatment. The court held that informed consent means that the patient has been fully informed about the nature, purpose, and consequences of the treatment or procedure, and has voluntarily agreed to undergo the same.

Note: When seeking consent to treatment, the question of whether the information given to a patient is adequate is judged from the perspective of a reasonable person in the patient's position.

In Montgomery vs Lanarkshire Health Board [2015] UKSC 11, a Scottish Court established a patient's right to receive information about the risks involved in a medical procedure. The decision emphasized the importance of informed consent, which is a fundamental right of a patient. The judgment has influenced medical law and practice worldwide, including in India.

In India, the Supreme Court has recognized the right to informed consent in various cases, including Samira Kohli vs Dr. Prabha Manchanda decided on 16 January, 2008. In this case, the Court held that "the patient has an absolute right to know about the pros and cons, the alternatives, and the likely consequences of a proposed treatment."

Moreover, the decision in Montgomery vs Lanarkshire Health Board has also been relied upon in consumer disputes before the Consumer Commissions. For instance, the National Consumer Disputes Redressal Commission (NCDRC) in India, in the case of Dr. S.K. Sama Vs. National Insurance Co. Ltd., held that a doctor has a duty to disclose all material risks involved in a medical procedure to the patient.

Therefore, the decision in Montgomery vs Lanarkshire Health Board has had a significant impact on Indian medical law and practice. The Indian courts and consumer commissions have recognized and implemented the principles laid down in this case to protect the rights of patients and ensure that patients are adequately informed before making decisions about their medical treatment.

The law relating to Informed Consent with effect from 2nd August 2023:

The National Medical Commission Registered Medical Practitioner (Professional Conduct) Regulations, 2023 has introduced the concept of informed consent in Regulation 19 with effect from 2nd August 2023. This is reproduced below:

19. Informed Consent:

(A). Before performing any clinical procedure, diagnostic or therapeutic, or operation, the RMP should obtain the signed documented informed consent of the patient. In case the patient is unable to give consent, the consent of the legal guardian or family member must be taken. The name of the operating surgeon must be mentioned in the medical records. In an operation that may result in sterility, the consent of both husband and wife is required. In case of an emergency, the doctor should try to obtain consent, but if this is not possible, he must act in the best interest of the patient. The medical records should describe the basis of decisions taken in an emergency No act of in-vitro fertilization or artificial insemination shall be undertaken without the informed written consent of the female patient and her spouse as well as the donor. (Consent Guidelines) (L4)

(B). RMP shall not publish photographs or case reports of patients without their consent/permission in any medical or another journal in any manner by which their identity could be revealed. (L1)

(C). Clinical drug trials or other research involving patients or volunteers must comply with ICMR guidelines and the New Drugs and Clinical Trials Rules, 2018. Consent taken from any patient or participant for the trial of drug or therapy which is not as per the guidelines shall be construed as misconduct. (Research Guidelines) (L2 and/or L4)

20. Conduct of RMP on Social/Electronic and Print Media shall follow the prescribed guidelines (Social Media Guidelines) (L1) 21. RMP should take due care in practice and exercise reasonable skills as expected, to preserve the life and health of the patient and follow the guidelines (Guidelines on Reasonable Care and Skill) (L4)

Mental Illnesses & Mediclaim Cover

An important issue relates to the treatment of mental diseases. Whether these are covered by the mediclaim or health insurance policies of insurance companies. Most mediclaim or health insurance policies specifically exclude the expenses incurred on treatment of mental diseases and reject claims relating to such treatments.

In a major report released on 17th June 2022, the World Health Organization (WHO) has estimated that one in every eight individuals worldwide suffers from a mental disorder, urging for immediate action to change mental healthcare. The WHO report says that by the end of 2022, about 20% of Indians would suffer from mental diseases.

This matter was considered in detail and decided by the Delhi High Court in Shikha Nischal vs National Insurance Company on 19 April, 2021. In this case, Shikha Nischal, the Petitioner, developed a certain illness for which she obtained treatment from Sukoon Hospital, Gurugram. She was admitted in the hospital on 28th June 2020 and discharged on 28th July 2020, after a month of treatment. The total expenses for the said period of hospitalization incurred by her was Rs. 5,54,636/-. She was diagnosed with Schizoaffective Disorder - a mental illness. She applied to National Insurance Company Limited for reimbursement of the expenses incurred in her treatment, amounting to Rs. 5,54,636/-.

By letter dated 1 September 2020, relying upon Clause 4.10 of the Healthcare Policy, the National Insurance Company Limited rejected her claim. The said Clause specifies the exclusions in respect of which the insurance company would not be liable to make payments under the Healthcare Policy. Clause 4.10 reads as under:

"4 - Exclusions: The company shall not be liable to make any payment under the policy, in respect of any expenses incurred in connection with or in respect of- … 4.10 - Psychiatric disorder, intentional self-inflicted injury: Treatment for all psychiatric and psychosomatic disorders/diseases, intentional self-inflicted injury, attempted suicide."

Shikha Nischal then filed a complaint before the Insurance Ombudsman relying upon the provisions of Mental Health Care Act

(MHA) 2017. The Insurance Ombudsman however, observed that the claim of the Petitioner would have to be settled in terms of the Clauses of the Healthcare Policy and rejected her claim.

She then approached the Delhi High Court. The short question before the Court was "Can mental illness be treated differently from physical illness for medical insurance purposes?"

However, during the hearing before the Delhi High Court, the Insurance Regulatory and Development Authority of India (IRDAI) directed National Insurance Company Limited to pay the claim of the Petitioner. Since the maximum coverage of the Healthcare Policy was only Rs. 3,95,000/-, National Insurance Company Limited paid Rs. 3,95,000/-, to the Petitioner.

The High Court observed that the present petition raises issues of grave public importance. It went into the matter in great detail and held that mental illness cannot be treated differently from other physical illnesses.

I am summarizing the Hon'ble High Court's important observations:

The United Nations recognized that in the modern world, mental health is as important as physical health and adopted the United Nations Convention on Rights of People with Disabilities which prohibited any form of discrimination in respect of mental illnesses or any other disabilities. The Convention recognizes mental disabilities as a form of disability and enshrines the principle of 'non-discrimination' towards such disabilities. The Convention has been ratified by India on 1st October, 2007.

Para 14 of the Judgment

The Convention not only recognizes the need for non- discrimination qua disabilities but also specifically refers to medical insurance, under Article 25, in particular.

The said Article reads as under:

"Article 25: Health States Parties recognize that persons with disabilities have the right to the enjoyment of the highest attainable standard of health without discrimination on the basis of disability. States Parties shall take all appropriate measures to ensure access for persons with disabilities to health services that are gender sensitive, including health- related rehabilitation. In particular, States Parties shall: ....

(e) Prohibit discrimination against persons with disabilities in the

provision of health insurance, and life insurance where such insurance is permitted by national law, which shall be provided in a fair and reasonable manner;" The spirit of the Convention, thus, ought to be reflected in the domestic regime in respect of mental healthcare.

Para 14 of the Judgment

Post-independence, the Mental Health Care Act, 1987 was the first statute dealing with mental illnesses. In order to bring the domestic law in line with the applicable United Nations Convention, the Mental Healthcare Bill, 2016 was promulgated which finally led to the enactment of Mental Health Care Act, 2017. The stated object of the Bill is "to provide for mental healthcare and services for persons with mental illness and to protect, promote and fulfil the rights of such persons during delivery of mental healthcare and services and matters connected therewith or incidental thereto".

Para 16 of the Judgment

The Mental Health Care Act, 2017 has a specific provision, being Section 21, which recognizes the right to equality and prohibits discrimination qua mental illnesses. Section 21 of the Mental Health Care Act, 2017 reads as under:

"21. (1) Every person with mental illness shall be treated as equal to persons with physical illness in the provision of all healthcare which shall include the following:-

there shall be no discrimination on any basis including gender, sex, sexual orientation, religion, culture, caste, social or political beliefs, class or disability;

(b) emergency facilities and emergency services for mental illness shall be of the same quality and availability as those provided to persons with physical illness;

(c) persons with mental illness shall be entitled to the use of ambulance services in the same manner, extent and quality as provided to persons with physical illness;

(d) living conditions in health establishments shall be of the same manner, extent and quality as provided to persons with physical illness; and

(e) any other health services provided to persons with physical illness shall be provided in same manner, extent and quality to persons with mental illness.

Para 17 of the Judgment

Every insurer shall make provision for medical insurance for treatment of mental illness on the same basis as is available for treatment of physical illness.

A perusal of the provisions of Mental Health Care Act, 2017 clearly shows that insurance companies had to make provision for mediclaim insurance for treatment of mental illnesses on the same basis as treatment available for physical illnesses. The Mental Health Care Act, 2017 was notified with effect from 7th July, 2018...... there is no doubt that the Mental Health Care Act, 2017 and its provisions, have been in effect since 2018.

Para 22 of the Judgment

It is clear from a perusal of the provisions of Mental Health Care Act, 2017, as also the provisions of the IRDAI Act, 1999 that immediately upon the Mental Health Care Act, 2017 coming into force, all insurance products ought to have extended the same treatment for mental and physical illnesses and remove any clause that discriminate between the same. The Insurance Ombudsman's order in the present case which holds that the provisions of the Mental Health Care Act are not relevant to the present Petitioner is untenable. The Mental Health Care Act, 2017 has come into effect from May/July, 2018, and thus the exclusion in the Healthcare Policy of National Insurance Company Limited with respect to "all psychiatric and psychosomatic disorders/ diseases", under Clause 4.10 as noted above, is contrary to law.

Para 27 of the Judgment

The summary of this important and well-reasoned decision is that "mental illness cannot be treated differently from other physical illness for medical insurance purposes *even if they are specifically excluded in the insurance policy*". And this stand has been confirmed by the IRDI and the National Insurance Company Limited.

Remedies available to the aggrieved Patient

Remedies available to the aggrieved Patient or his Representative

The following four remedies are available to the aggrieved person:

1. Civil suit for damages in a Civil Court which is expensive and time-consuming.

2. Complaint for damages under the Consumer Protection Act (this is the easiest and most preferred remedy). But now this is also taking a long time.

3. Complaint with the State Medical Council.

4. Criminal Case for negligence (this is rather rare but far more serious).

Civil Liability – Claim for damages

The aggrieved persons have the option of filing cases for compensation either in a Civil Court or under the Consumer Protection Act. The Civil Court is more expensive and cumbersome.

The Consumer Commissions take lesser time, the fee is nominal and the procedure is far simpler.

Complaint under the Consumer Protection Act, 2019

(The old Consumer Protection Act of 1986 has been replaced by the new Consumer Protection Act, 2019. But the principles involved remain the same).

Any person filing a Complaint under the Consumer Protection Act has to be a Consumer.

Who is a Consumer? In the case of Doctors and Nursing Homes, a Consumer is a person who pays for medical services. This had become a very complicated issue because there are paying patients, Clinical Establishments (Registration and Regulation) Act, 2010.

there are free patients, there are Govt. Hospitals and non-govt. Hospitals, etc. Finally, the Supreme Court decided the matter. The Supreme Court considered cases of treatment in Govt. hospitals and non Govt. hospitals. It also considered cases where fees are paid by the patients as well as cases where no fee is paid by the patients. In this case, the Supreme Court heard a number of appeals, Special Leave Petitions and a Writ Petition raising a common question, viz., whether and, if so, in what circumstances, a medical practitioner can be regarded as rendering 'service' under Section 2(1)(o) of the Consumer Protection Act, 1986.

Connected with this issue was the question whether the service rendered at a hospital/nursing home can be regarded as 'service' under Section 2(1)(o) of the Act.

The patient will be able to file a Complaint under the Consumer Protection Act only if such service can be regarded as 'service' under Section 2(1)(o) of the Consumer Protection Act. These questions had been considered by various High Courts as well as by the National Consumer Disputes Redressal Commission. The issue was argued and discussed at length and finally decided by the Supreme Court. The Supreme Court laid down the law in which type of cases the aggrieved patients could file a complaint under the Consumer Protection Act, 1986. I am giving the gist of the decision.

"On the basis of the above discussion the Judges arrive at the following conclusions:

(1) Service rendered to a patient by a medical practitioner (except where the doctor renders service free of charge to every patient or under a contract of personal service), by way of consultation, diagnosis and treatment, both medicinal and surgical, would fall within the ambit of 'service' as defined in Section 2(1)(o) of the Act.

Note : Where the patient pays fees, he is a Consumer and can file a Complaint under the Consumer Protection Act.

(2) The fact that medical practitioners belong to the medical profession and are subject to the disciplinary control of the Medical Council of India and/or State Medical Councils constituted under the provisions of the Indian Medical Council Act would not exclude the services rendered by them from the ambit of the Act.

Note : The fact that doctors are subject to disciplinary control of the Medical Council of India and/or State Medical Councils does not make any difference. The patient can file a complaint both under the Consumer Protection Act as well as with the Medical Council of India and/or State Medical Council.

(3) A 'contract of personal service' has to be distinguished from a 'contract for personal services'. In the absence of a relationship of master and servant between the patient and medical practitioner, the service rendered by a medical practitioner to the patient would fall within the ambit of 'service' as defined in Section 2(1)(o) of the Act.

Note : Where the patient pays fees, he is a Consumer and can file a Complaint under the Consumer Protections Act. But if a Doctor is an employee of the patient, then he cannot file a Complaint under the Consumer Protection Act.

(4) The expression 'contract of personal service' in Section 2(1)

(o) of the Act cannot be confined to contracts for employment of domestic servants only and the said expression would include the employment of a medical officer for the purpose of rendering medical service to the employer. The service rendered by a medical officer to his employer under the contract of employment would be outside the purview of 'service' as defined in Section 2(1) (o) of the Act.

Note : Where the patient pays fees, he is a Consumer and can file a Complaint under the Consumer Protections Act. But if the Doctor is an employee of the patient, then he cannot file a Complaint under the Consumer Protection Act.

(5)   Service rendered free of charge by a medical practitioner attached to a hospital/Nursing home or a medical officer employed in a hospital/Nursing home where such services are rendered free of charge to everybody, would not be "service" as defined in Section 2(1)(o) of the Act. The payment of a token amount for registration purpose only at the hospital/nursing home would not alter the position.

Note : Where Services are rendered free in a hospital/Nursing home and such services are rendered free of charge to everybody – a Patient can not file a Complaint under the Consumer Protection Act even though the Patient has paid a token registration fee.

6)   Service rendered at a non-Government hospital/Nursing home where no charge whatsoever is made from any person availing the service and all patients (rich and poor) are given free service - is outside the purview of the expression 'service' as defined in Section 2(1) (o) of the Act. The payment of a token amount for registration purpose only at the hospital/Nursing home would not alter the position.

Note : Where Services are rendered free in a non-Govt. hospital

/Nursing home where such services are rendered free of charge to everybody – the patient can not file a Complaint under the Consumer Protection Act even though the Patient has paid a token registration fee.

(7)   Service rendered at a non-Government hospital/Nursing home where charges are required to be paid by the persons availing such services falls within the purview of the expression 'service' as defined in Section 2(1) (o) of the Act.

Note : Where Services are rendered on payment of charges in a non- Govt. hospital/Nursing home – the patient can file a Complaint under the Consumer Protection Act.

(8)   Service rendered at a non-Government hospital/Nursing home where charges are required to be paid by persons who are

in a position to pay and persons who cannot afford to pay are rendered service free of charge would fall within the ambit of the expression 'service' as defined in section 2(1) (o) of the Act irrespective of the fact that the service is rendered free of charge to persons who are not in a position to pay for such services. Free service, would also be "service" and the recipient a "consumer" under the Act.

Note : Where Services are rendered in a non-Govt. hospital/Nursing home on payment of charges for those who can afford to pay and free for those who cannot pay — even patients who are getting free treatment can file a Complaint under the Consumer Protection Act.

(9) Service rendered at a Government hospital/health centre/ dispensary where no charge whatsoever is made from any person availing the services and all patients (rich and poor) are given free service - is outside the purview of the expression 'service' as defined in Section 2(1) (o) of the Act. The payment of a token amount for registration purpose only at the hospital/nursing home would not alter the position.

Note : Where Services are rendered in a Government hospital/health centre/dispensary free of charge to everybody — a patient can not file a Complaint under the Consumer Protection Act even though the Patient has paid a token registration fee.

(10) Service rendered at a Government hospital/health centre/ dispensary where services are rendered on payment of charges and also rendered free of charge to other persons availing such services would fall within the ambit of the expression 'service' as defined in Section 2(1)(o) of the Act irrespective of the fact that the service is rendered free of charge to persons who do not pay for such service. Free service would also be "service" and the recipient a "consumer" under the Act.

Note : Where Services are rendered in a Government hospital/health centre/dispensary on payment of charges for those who can afford to pay and free for those who cannot pay – even Patients who are getting free treatment can file a Complaint under the Consumer Protection Act.

(11)Service rendered by a medical practitioner or hospital/nursing home cannot be regarded as service rendered free of charge, if the person availing the service has taken an insurance policy for medical care where under the charges for consultation, diagnosis and medical treatment are borne by the insurance company, such service would fall within the ambit of 'service' as defined in Section 2(1) (o) of the Act.

Note : Where Services are rendered by a medical practitioner or hospital/ nursing home and the charges are reimbursed by an insurance company - patients who are getting the treatment can file a Complaint under the Consumer Protection Act.

(12) Similarly, where, as a part of the conditions of service, the employer bears the expenses of medical treatment of an employee and his family members dependent on him, the service rendered to such an employee and his family members by a medical practitioner or a hospital/nursing home would not be free of charge and would constitute 'service' under Section 2(1)(o) of the Act.

Note : Where Services are rendered by a medical practitioner or hospital/nursing home and the charges are reimbursed by the employer – patients who are getting the treatment can file a Complaint under the Consumer Protection Act.

Indian Medical Association Vs. V.P. Shantha & Ors. decided on 13 November 1995

Anuradha Saha case – highest ever compensation for medical negligence paid in India

Mrs. Anuradha Saha, aged about 36 years, and her husband, Dr. Kunal Saha visited India on a holiday in 1998. Anuradha fell victim to a rare disease - toxic epidermal necrolysis (TEN). On 11 May 1998, she was admitted to Advanced Medicare & Research Institute hospital (AMRI) in Kolkata.

"When Dr. Sukumar Mukherjee examined Anuradha, she had rashes all over her body and this being the case of dermatology, he should have referred her to a dermatologist. Instead, he prescribed "Depomedrol" for the next 3 days on his assumption that it was a case of "vasculitis". (Depomedrol is an anti-inflammatory glucocorticoid for intramuscular, intra-articular, soft tissue or intra-lesional injection and is used to treat many different inflammatory conditions such as arthritis, lupus, psoriasis, ulcerative colitis, allergic disorders, etc.)

The dosage of 120 mg Depomedrol per day is certainly a higher dose in case of a TEN patient or for that matter any patient suffering from any other bypass or skin disease and the maximum recommended usage by the drug manufacturer has also been exceeded by Dr. Mukherjee. On 11 May 1998, he further prescribed Depomedrol without diagnosing the nature of the disease   .....

"In the morning of 11 May 1998 under Dr. Mukherjee's supervision, Anuradha was also examined by Dr. Baidyanath Halder ..... Dr. Halder found that she had been suffering from erythema plus blisters. Her condition, however, continued to deteriorate further. Dr. Abani Roy Chowdhury, Consultant was also consulted on 12 May 1998.

"On or about 17 May 1998, Anuradha was shifted to Breach Candy Hospital, Mumbai by air ambulance as her condition further deteriorated severely. She breathed her last on 28 May 1998......"

Dr. Kunal Saha filed a complaint under the Consumer Protection Act 1968 before the National Consumer Disputes Redressal Commission (NCDRC) on 9 March 1999. Not satisfied with the decision of the NCDRC, he preferred appeal to the Supreme Court of India. After hearing the case, the Supreme Court remanded the case back to the NCDRC for determining the quantum of compensation to be paid by AMRI and three Kolkata doctors.

The NCDRC rejected more than 98% of the total original claim of Rs. 77.7 crores which was modified to Rs. 97.5 crores later on, by adding "special damages" due to further economic loss, loss of employment, bankruptcy, etc. suffered by the claimant in the course of the 5-year long trial. The NCDRC awarded compensation of only Rs.1.3 crores after reducing from the total award of Rs.1.72 crores on the ground that the claimant had "interfered" in the treatment of his wife and since one of the guilty doctors had already expired, his share of compensation was also denied.

Dr. Kunal Saha appealed to the Supreme Court against the order of the NCDRC and the 15-year-long litigation ended on 24 October 2013 when the Supreme Court enhanced the compensation awarded by the NCDRC to Rs.6,08,00,550/- with interest of 6% per annum from the date of the complaint to the date of the payment to the claimant.

The Supreme Court awarded total compensation of Rs. 6,08,00,550/- under different heads as under:

Loss of income of the deceased   Rs. 5,72,00,550/-

For Medical treatment in Kolkata
and Mumbai   Rs. 7,00,000/-
Travel and Hotel expenses at Mumbai   Rs. 6,50,000/-

Loss of consortium   Rs. 1,00,000/-
Pain and suffering   Rs. 10,00,000/-
Cost of litigation   Rs. 11,50,000/-

"147. Therefore, a total amount of Rs.6,08,00,550/- is the compen- sation awarded in this appeal to the claimant Dr. Kunal Saha by partly modifying the award granted by the National Commission under different heads with 6% interest per annum from the date of application till the date of payment."

(The main reason for the award of the huge damages is that it was calculated in US $.)

The Supreme Court Judges were not happy with the behaviour of the Doctors. They made scathing comments.

"148. Before parting with the judgment we are inclined to mention that the number of medical negligence cases against doctors, Hospitals and Nursing Homes in the consumer forum are increasing day by day. In the case of Paschim Banga Khet Mazdoor Samity Vs. State of West Bengal, this Court has already pronounced that right to health of a citizen is a fundamental right guaranteed under Article 21 of the Constitution of India. It was held in that case that all the government Hospitals, Nursing Homes and Poly-clinics are liable to provide treatment to the best of their capacity to all the patients.

"149. The doctors, Hospitals, the Nursing Homes and other connected establishments are to be dealt with strictly if they are found to be negligent with the patients who come to them pawning all their money with the hope to live a better life with dignity. The patients irrespective of their social, cultural and economic background are entitled to be treated with dignity which not only forms their fundamental right but also their human right. We, therefore, hope and trust that this decision acts as a deterrent and a reminder to those doctors, Hospitals, the Nursing Homes and other connected establishments who do not take their responsibility seriously.

"150. The central and the state governments may consider enacting laws wherever there is absence of one for effective functioning of the private Hospitals and Nursing Homes. Since the conduct of doctors is already regulated by the Medical Council of India, we hope and trust for impartial and strict scrutiny from the body. Finally, we hope and believe that the institutions and individuals providing medical services to the public at large educate and update themselves about any new medical discipline and rare diseases so as to avoid tragedies such as the instant case where a valuable life could have been saved with a little more awareness and wisdom from the part of the doctors and the Hospital."

Balram Prasad vs Kunal Saha & Ors (SC) decided on 24 October, 2013

Another important Decision

The parents of a 6-year-old child took him to Sankara Nethralaya, Chennai where doctors suggested a minor squint eye surgery. The boy was referred to Senior Surgeon, Dr. T.S. Surendran. He scheduled the surgery on 14 June 2000. On the day before the surgery, the Physician Dr. Sujatha examined the boy. She noticed a faint functional systolic 'murmur' and chest wall abnormality. She brought it to the notice of the Senior Cardiologist, Dr. S. Bhaskaran. He examined the child and after conducting some exercises, concluded that there was no murmur. Dr. S. Bhaskaran also ruled out the necessity for further tests like ECG, ECHO or Chest X-ray, and declared the child was 'Fit for General Anesthesia'.

The child was brought to the hospital on empty stomach on the scheduled date and taken to the Operation Theatre only at 2 P.M. after a gap of 9 hours and 20 minutes of fasting which led the child to be hypoglycemic, a potential cardiac arrest threat. The child died.

Another allegation was that Halothane was used as an anaesthetic agent which was known to cause Bradycardia - a slow heart rate. The hearts of adults at rest usually beat between 60 and 100 times a minute. In bradycardia, the heart beats fewer than 60 times a minute. Normally, Atropine is administered as a pre-medication to prevent the same.

The parents of the child alleged that the child had not been administered the right dose and that there had been a huge gap of time between atropinization and actual surgery. It was also pointed out the Senior Surgeon could have postponed the child's surgery as he had already completed 16 surgeries that very day and the child was not requiring any imminent attention. The parents of the deceased child filed a complaint under Section 21 of the Consumer Protection Act, 1986 against Sankara Nethralaya Hospital, Senior Surgeon Dr. T.S. Surendran, and Anaesthetist, Dr. Kannan. They claimed compensation of 1,00,20,000/-

The National Consumer Disputes Redressal Commission (NCDRC) held that the expected degree of skill from a Cardiologist was more and a higher degree of care was expected. The NCDRC held that the Anesthetist should have warned the operating surgeon. Patients who are considered at risk for OCR should warrant particular attention. NCDRC also found merit in the contention that the surgery could have been postponed.

NCDRC held the Cardiologist, the Operating surgeon, and the Anesthetist liable for negligence for having failed to exercise their duty of care with the required ordinary skills and standards. Based on the Supreme Court decision in National Insurance Co Ltd v. Kusum about the payment of compensation to parents for the death of a child, NCDRC regarded Rs. 1 Crore compensation 'just and fair' and awarded compensation of Rs.

1 Crore to the parents.

Dr. Reba Modak & Anr. vs. Sankara Nethralaya & Ors. National Consumer Disputes Redressal Commission date of order 26 August 2022

Another interesting case of compensation for Medical Negligence

A child became blind due to the negligence of the doctors. The Supreme Court observed as follows:

"11.2.1 As per medical literature, all infants with a birth weight of less than 1500 grams, or gestational age of less than 32 weeks, are required to be mandatorily screened for ROP, which usually takes about 4 to 5 weeks to be diagnosed. The routine screening should begin no later than 4 weeks after birth, and possibly even earlier for infants at higher risk (2 to 3 weeks). The standard of care is to be judged in the light of the protocols and standard procedures prevailing on the date of birth, and not on the date of trial."

The Supreme Court ordered compensation of Rs. 76,00,000/-.

Maharaja Agrasen Hospital&Ors Versus Master Rishabh Sharma & Ors. (SC) decided on 16 December 2019

Complaint with the State Medical Council

All doctors have to be registered with the State Medical Council. They are covered by the provisions of the National Medical Commission Registered Medical Practitioner (Professional Conduct) Regulations, 2023 with effect from 2nd August 2023. Any aggrieved person, including a patient, can file a complaint against a Doctor for Medical Negligence (or any other Professional misconduct) and the State Medical Council can take disciplinary action against the Doctor, which includes permanent debar from practice. However, the State Medical Council cannot award damages or compensation, or any other form of monetary compensation.

Some instances of Professional misconduct are enumerated in the Regulations. But there can be other forms of Professional misconduct - such as false advertisement, taking benefits from manufacturers of medicine, taking commission from pathological laboratories, etc.

Criminal Liability

An unfortunate period came when aggrieved persons started filing criminal complaints against doctors for Medical Negligence under various sections of the Indian Penal Code. This was a bad trend and doctors were scared in taking decisions in serious cases. The Supreme Court came to their rescue.

On 15.2.1995, late Jiwan Lal Sharma, the Complainant's father, was admitted as a patient in a private ward of CMC Hospital, Ludhiana. On 22.2.1995, at about 11 p.m. Jiwan Lal felt difficulty in breathing. The Complainant's elder brother, Vijay Sharma, who was present in the room, contacted the duty nurse, who in turn called some doctor to attend to the patient. No doctor turned up for about 20 to 25 minutes.

Then, Dr. Jacob Mathew, and Dr. Allen Joseph came to the room of the patient. An oxygen cylinder was brought and connected to the mouth of the patient, but the breathing problem increased further. The patient tried to get up but the medical staff asked him to remain in the bed. The oxygen cylinder was found to be empty. There was no other gas cylinder available in the room.

Vijay Sharma went to the adjoining room and brought a gas cylinder from there. However, there was no arrangement to make the gas cylinder functional. Between 5 to 7 minutes were wasted. By this time, another doctor came who declared that the patient was dead.

The Complainant filed FIR that: "the death of my father was occurred due to the carelessness of doctors and nurses and non-availability of oxygen cylinder and the empty cylinder was fixed on the mouth of my father and his breathing was totally stopped hence my father died. I sent the dead body of my father to my village for last cremation and for information I have come to you. Suitable action be done

Sd/- ──────

As per statement of intimator, the death of Jiwan Lal Sharma has occurred due to carelessness of doctors and nurses concerned and to fit empty gas cylinder. On the above report, an offence under Section 304A/34 IPC was registered and investigated. The matter finally went up to the Supreme Court.

The Supreme Court held that the legal concept of negligence is different in civil and criminal law. What may be negligence in civil law may not necessarily be negligence in criminal law. For negligence to amount to an offence, the element of mens rea must be shown to exist.

It observed as follows:

"A medical practitioner faced with an emergency ordinarily tries his best to redeem the patient out of his suffering. He does not gain anything by acting with negligence or by omitting to do an act. Obviously, therefore, it will be for the complainant to clearly make out a case of negligence before a medical practitioner is charged with or proceeded against criminally.   A surgeon with shaky hands under fear of legal action cannot perform a successful operation and a quivering physician cannot administer the end-dose of medicine to his patient. If the hands be trembling with the dangling fear of facing a criminal prosecution in the event of failure for whatever reason - whether attributable to himself or not, neither a surgeon can successfully wield his life-saving scalpel to perform an essential surgery, nor can a physician successfully administer the life-saving dose of medicine. Discretion being better part of valour, a medical professional would feel better advised to leave a terminal patient to his own fate in the case of emergency where the chance of success may be 10% (or so), rather than taking the risk of making a last ditch effort towards saving the subject and facing a criminal prosecution if his effort fails. Such timidity forced upon a doctor would be a disservice to the society.

"The jurisprudential concept of negligence differs in civil and criminal law. What may be negligence in civil law may not necessarily be negligence in criminal law. For negligence to amount to an offence, the element of mens rea must be shown to exist. For an act to amount to criminal negligence, the degree of negligence should be much higher i.e. gross or of a very high degree. Negligence which is neither gross nor of a higher degree may provide a ground for action in civil law but cannot form the basis for prosecution.

"Guidelines - re: prosecuting medical professionals. As we have noticed hereinabove that the cases of doctors (surgeons and physicians) being subjected to criminal prosecution are on an increase. Sometimes such prosecutions are filed by private complainants and sometimes by police on an FIR being lodged and cognizance taken. The investigating officer and the private complainant cannot always be supposed to have knowledge of medical science so as to determine whether the act of the accused medical professional amounts to rash or negligent act within the domain of criminal law under Section 304-A of IPC.

The criminal process once initiated subjects the medical professional to serious embarrassment and sometimes harassment. He has to seek bail to escape arrest, which may or may not be granted to him. At the end he may be exonerated by acquittal or discharge but the loss which he has suffered in his reputation cannot be compensated by any standards.

"Many a complainant prefers recourse to criminal process as a tool for pressurizing the medical professional for extracting un-called for or unjust compensation. Such malicious proceedings have to be guarded against.

"A private complaint may not be entertained unless the complainant has produced prima facie evidence before the Court in the form of a credible opinion given by another competent doctor to support the charge of rashness or negligence on the part of the accused doctor. The investigating officer should, before proceeding against the doctor accused of rash or negligent act or omission, obtain an independent and competent medical opinion preferably from a doctor in government service qualified in that branch of medical practice who can normally be expected to give an impartial and unbiased opinion applying Bolam's test to the facts collected in the investigation. A doctor accused of rashness or negligence, may not be arrested in a routine manner (simply because a charge has been levelled against him). Unless his arrest is necessary for furthering the investigation or for collecting evidence or unless the investigation officer feels satisfied that the doctor proceeded against would not make himself available to face the prosecution unless arrested, the arrest may be withheld.

"Reverting back to the facts of the case before us, we are satisfied that all the averments made in the complaint, even if held to be proved, do not make out a case of criminal rashness or negligence on the part of the accused…"

The Supreme Court quashed the criminal proceedings.

Jacob Mathew v. State of Punjab (SC) decided on *05/08/2005*

The National Medical Commission Act 2019

ARRANGEMENT OF SECTIONS

SECTIONS

CHAPTER III- THE MEDICAL ADVISORY COUNCIL

CHAPTER IV- NATIONAL EXAMINATION

CHAPTER V - AUTONOMOUS BOARDS

SECTIONS

CHAPTER VI - RECOGNITION OF MEDICAL QUALIFICATIONS

CHAPTER VII - GRANTS, AUDIT AND ACCOUNTS

CHAPTER VIII - MISCELLANEOUS

SECTIONS

THE SCHEDULE

THE NATIONAL MEDICAL COMMISSION ACT, 2019 ACT NO. 30 OF 2019

[*8th August*, 2019.]

An Act to provide for a medical education system that improves access to quality and affordable medical education, ensures availability of adequate and high quality medical professionals in all parts of the country; that promotes equitable and universal healthcare that encourages community health perspective and makes services of medical professionals accessible to all the citizens; that promotes national health goals; that encourages medical professionals to adopt latest medical research in their work and to contribute to research; that has an objective periodic and transparent assessment of medical institutions and facilitates maintenance of a medical register for India and enforces high ethical standards in all aspects of medical services; that is flexible to adapt to changing needs and has an effective grievance redressal mechanism and for matters connected therewith or incidental thereto.

BE it enacted by Parliament in the Seventieth Year of the Republic of India as follows:—

CHAPTER I PRELIMINARY

1.   Short title, extent and commencement.—(*1*) This Act may be called the National Medical Commission Act, 2019.

(2)   It extends to the whole of India.

(3)   It shall come into force on such date[1] as the Central Government may, by notification in the Official Gazette, appoint, and different dates may be appointed for different provisions of this Act andany reference in any such provision to the commencement of this

Act shall be construed as a reference to the coming into force of that provision.

2.   Definitions.—In this Act, unless the context otherwise requires,—

(a)   "Autonomous Board" means any of the Autonomous Boards constituted under section 16;

(b)   "Chairperson" means the Chairperson of the National Medical Commission appointed under section 5;

(c)   "Commission" means the National Medical Commission constituted under section 3;

(d)   "Council" means the Medical Advisory Council constituted under section 11;

(e)   "Ethics and Medical Registration Board" means the Board constituted under section 16;

(f)   "health University" means a University specialised in affiliating institutions engaged in teaching medicine, medical and health sciences and includes a medical University and University of health sciences;

(g)   "licence" means a licence to practice medicine granted under sub-section (*1*) of section 33;

(h)   "Medical Assessment and Rating Board" means the Board constituted under section 16;

1. 2nd September, 2019—Sections 3, 4, 5, 6, 8, 11, 16, 17, 18, 19, 56 and 57, *vide* notification No. S.O. 3162(E), dated 2ndSeptember, 2019, *see* Gazette of India, Extraordinary, Part II, sec. 3(*ii*).

25th September, 2020—all the remaining provisions, *vide* notification No. S.O. 3262(E), dated 24th September, 2020, *see*

Gazette of India, Extraordinary, Part II, sec. 3, Sub-section(*ii*) .

(i)   "medical institution" means any institution within or outside India which grants degrees, diplomas or licences in medicine and include affiliated colleges and deemed to be Universities;

(j)   "medicine" means modern scientific medicine in all its branches and includes surgery and obstetrics, but does not include veterinary medicine and surgery;

(k)   "Member" means a Member of the Commission appointed under section 5 and includes the Chairperson thereof;

(l)   "National Board of Examination" means the body registered as such under the Societies Registration Act, 1860 (21 of 1860) which grants broad-speciality and super-speciality qualifications referred to in the Schedule;

(m)   "National Register" means a National Medical Register maintained by the Ethics and MedicalRegistration Board under section 31;

(n)   "notification" means notification published in the Official Gazette and the expression "notify"shall be construed accordingly;

(o)   "Post-Graduate Medical Education Board" means the Board constituted under section 16;

(p)   "prescribed" means prescribed by rules made under this Act;

(q)   "President" means the President of an Autonomous Board appointed under section 18;

(r)   "recognised medical qualification" means a medical qualification recognised under section 35 or section 36 or section 37 or section 40, as the case may be;

(s)   "regulations" means the regulations made by the Commission under this Act;

(t)   "Schedule" means the Schedule to this Act;

(u)   "State Medical Council" means a medical council constituted under any law for the timebeing in force in any State or Union territory for regulating the practice and registration of practitioners of medicine in that State or Union territory;

(v)   "State Register" means a register maintained under any law for the time being in force in any State or Union territory for registration of practitioners of medicine;

(w)   "Under-Graduate Medical Education Board" means the Board constituted under section 16;

(x)   "University" shall have the same meaning as assigned to it in clause (*f*) of section 2 of the University Grants Commission Act, 1956 (3 of 1956) and includes a health University.

CHAPTER II - THE NATIONAL MEDICAL COMMISSION

3.   Constitution of National Medical Commission.—(*1*) The Central Government shall constitute a Commission, to be known as the National Medical Commission, to exercise the powers conferred upon, and to perform the functions assigned to it, under this Act.

(2)   The Commission shall be a body corporate by the name aforesaid, having perpetual succession and a common seal, with power, subject to the provisions of this Act, to acquire, hold and dispose of property, both movable and immovable, and to contract, and shall, by the said name, sue or be sued.

(3)   The head office of the Commission shall be at New Delhi.

4.   Composition of Commission.—(*1*) The Commission shall consist of the following persons to be appointed by the Central Government, namely:—

(a)   a Chairperson;

(b)   ten *ex officio* Members; and

(c)   twenty-two part-time Members.

(2)   The Chairperson shall be a medical professional of outstanding ability, proven administrative capacity and integrity, possessing a postgraduate degree in any discipline of medical sciences from any University and having experience of not less than twenty years in the field of medical sciences, out of which at least ten years shall be as a leader in the area of medical education.

(3)   The following persons shall be the *ex officio* Members of the Commission, namely:—

(a)   the President of the Under-Graduate Medical Education Board;

(b)   the President of the Post-Graduate Medical Education Board;

(c)   the President of the Medical Assessment and Rating Board;

(d)   the President of the Ethics and Medical Registration Board;

(e)   the Director General of Health Services, Directorate General of Health Services, New Delhi;

(f)   the Director General, Indian Council of Medical Research;

(g)   a Director of any of the All India Institutes of Medical Sciences, to be nominated by the Central Government;

(h)   two persons from amongst the Directors of Postgraduate Institute of Medical Education and Research, Chandigarh; Jawaharlal Institute of Postgraduate Medical Education and Research, Puducherry; Tata Memorial Hospital, Mumbai; North Eastern Indira Gandhi Regional Institute of Health and Medical Sciences, Shillong; and All India Institute of Hygiene and Public Health,

Kolkata; to be nominated by the Central Government; and

(i)   one person to represent the Ministry of the Central Government dealing with Health and Family Welfare, not below the rank of Additional Secretary to the Government of India, to be nominated by that Ministry.

(4)   The following persons shall be appointed as part-time Members of the Commission, namely:—

(a)   three Members to be appointed from amongst persons of ability, integrity and standing, who have special knowledge and professional experience in such areas including management, law, medical ethics, health research, consumer or patient rights advocacy, science and technology and economics;

(b)   ten Members to be appointed on rotational basis from amongst the nominees of the States and Union territories, under clauses (*c*) and (*d*) of sub-section (*2*) of section 11, in the Medical Advisory Council for a term of two years in such manner as may be prescribed;

(c)   nine members to be appointed from amongst the nominees of the States and Union territories, under clause (*e*) of sub-section (*2*) of section 11, in the Medical Advisory Council for a term of two years in such manner as may be prescribed.

Explanation.—For the purposes of this section and section 17, the term "leader" means the Headof a Department or the Head of an organisation.

5.   Search Committee for appointment of Chairperson and Members.—(*1*) The Central Government shall appoint the Chairperson, part-time Members referred to in clause (*a*) of sub-section (*4*) of section 4 and the Secretary referred to in section 8 on the recommendation of a Search Committee consisting of—

(a)   the Cabinet Secretary—Chairperson;

(b)   three experts, possessing outstanding qualifications and experience of not less than twenty- five years in the field of medical education, public health education and health research, to be nominated by the Central Government— Members;

(c)   one expert, from amongst the part-time Members referred to in clause (*c*) of sub-section (*4*) of section 4, to be nominated by the Central Government in such manner as may be prescribed— Member;

(d)   one person, possessing outstanding qualifications and experience of not less than twenty-five years in the field of management or law or economics or science and technology, to be nominated by the Central Government—Member; and

(e)   the Secretary to the Government of India in charge of the Ministry of Health and Family Welfare, to be the Convenor—Member.

(2)   The Central Government shall, within one month from the date of occurrence of any vacancy, including by reason of death, resignation or removal of the Chairperson or a Member, or within three months before the end of tenure of the Chairperson or Member, make a reference to the Search Committee for filling up of the vacancy.

(3)   The Search Committee shall recommend a panel of at least

three names for every vacancy referredto it.

(4)   The Search Committee shall, before recommending any person for appointment as the Chairperson or a Member of the Commission, satisfy itself that such person does not have any financial or other interest which is likely to affect prejudicially his functions as such Chairperson or Member.

(5)   No appointment of the Chairperson or Member shall be invalid merely by reason of any vacancy or absence of a Member in the Search Committee.

(6)   Subject to the provisions of sub-sections (2) to (5), the Search Committee may regulate its own procedure.

6.   Term of office and conditions of service of Chairperson and Members.—(1) The Chairperson and the part-time Members, other than the part-time Members appointed under clauses (b) and (c) of sub-section (4) of section 4, shall hold office for a term not exceeding four years and shall not be eligible for any extension or re-appointment:

Provided that such person shall cease to hold office after attaining the age of seventy years.

(2)   The term of office of an *ex officio* Member shall continue as long as he holds the office by virtue of which he is such Member.

(3)   Where a Member, other than an *ex officio* Member, is absent from three consecutive ordinary meetings of the Commission and the cause of such absence is not attributable to any valid reason in the opinion of the Commission, such Member shall be deemed to have vacated the seat.

The salaries and allowances payable to, and other terms and conditions of service of, the Chairperson and Member, other than an *ex officio* Member, shall be such as may be prescribed.

(4)   The Chairperson or a Member may,—

(a)   relinquish his office by giving in writing to the Central Government a notice of not less thanthree months; or

(b)   be removed from his office in accordance with the provisions of section 7:

Provided that such person may be relieved from duties earlier than three months or be allowed to continue beyond three months until a successor is appointed, if the Central Government so decides.

(5)   The Chairperson and every member of the Commission shall make declaration of his assets andhis liabilities at the time of entering upon his office and at the time of demitting his office and also declare his professional and commercial engagement or involvement in such form and manner as may beprescribed, and such declaration shall be published on the website of the Commission.

(6)   The Chairperson or a Member, ceasing to hold office as such, shall not accept, for a period of two years from the date of demitting such office, any employment, in any capacity, including as a consultant or an expert, in any private medical institution, whose matter has been dealt with by such Chairperson or Member, directly or indirectly:

Provided that nothing herein shall be construed as preventing such person from accepting an employment in a body or institution, including medical institution, controlled or maintained by the Central Government or a State Government:

Provided further that nothing herein shall prevent the Central Government from permitting theChairperson or a Member to accept any employment in any capacity, including as a consultant or expertin any private medical institution whose matter has been dealt with by such Chairperson or Member.

7.   Removal of Chairperson and Member of Commission.—
(*1*) The Central Government may, by order, remove from office the Chairperson or any other Member, who—

(a)   has been adjudged an insolvent; or

(b)   has been convicted of an offence which, in the opinion of the Central Government, involvesmoral turpitude; or

(c)   has become physically or mentally incapable of acting as a Member; or

(d)   is of unsound mind and stands so declared by a competent court; or

(e)   has acquired such financial or other interest as is likely to affect prejudicially his functions asa Member; or

(f)   has so abused his position as to render his continuance in office prejudicial to public interest.

(2) No Member shall be removed under clauses (*e*) and (*f*) of sub-section (*1*) unless he has been given a reasonable opportunity of being heard in the matter.

8.   Appointment of Secretary, experts, professionals, officers and other employees of Commission.—(*1*) There shall be a Secretariat for the Commission to be headed by a Secretary, to be appointed by the Central Government in accordance with the provisions of section 5.

(2)   The Secretary of the Commission shall be a person of proven administrative capacity andintegrity, possessing such qualifications and experience as may be prescribed.

(3)   The Secretary shall be appointed by the Central Government for a term of four years and shall not be eligible for any extension or re-appointment.

(4)   The Secretary shall discharge such functions of the Commission as are assigned to him by the Commission and as may be specified by regulations made under this Act.

(5)   The Commission may, for the efficient discharge of its functions under this Act, appoint such officers and other employees, as it considers necessary, against the posts created by the Central Government.

(6)   The salaries and allowances payable to, and other terms and conditions of service of, the Secretary, officers and other employees of the Commission shall be such as may be prescribed.

(7)   The Commission may engage, in accordance with the procedure specified by regulations, such number of experts and professionals of integrity and outstanding ability, who have special

knowledge of, and experience in such fields, including medical education, public health, management, health economics, quality assurance, patient advocacy, health research, science and technology, administration, finance, accounts and law, as it deems necessary, to assist the Commission in the discharge of its functions under this Act.

9.   Meetings, etc., of Commission.—(*1*) The Commission shall meet at least once every quarter at such time and place as may be appointed by the Chairperson.

(2)   The Chairperson shall preside at the meeting of the Commission, and if, for any reason, the Chairperson is unable to attend a meeting of the Commission, any other Member, being the President of an Autonomous Board, nominated by the Chairperson, shall preside at the meeting.

(3)   Unless the procedure to be followed at the meetings of the Commission is otherwise provided by regulations, one-half of the total number of Members of the Commission including the Chairperson shall constitute the quorum and all the acts of the Commission shall be decided by a majority of the members, present and voting and in the event of equality of votes, the Chairperson, or in his absence, the President of the Autonomous Board nominated under sub-section (*2*), shall have the casting vote.

(4)   The general superintendence, direction and control of the administration of the Commission shall vest in the Chairperson.

(5)   No act done by the Commission shall be questioned on the ground of the existence of a vacancy in, or a defect in the constitution of, the Commission.

(6)   A person who is aggrieved by any decision of the Commission except the decision rendered undersub-section (*4*) of section 30 may prefer an appeal to the Central Government against such decision withinthirty days of the communication of such decision.

10.   Powers and functions of Commission.—(*1*) The Commission shall perform the followingfunctions, namely:—

(a)   lay down policies for maintaining a high quality and high standards in medical education andmake necessary regulations in this behalf;

(b)   lay down policies for regulating medical institutions, medical researches and medical professionals and make necessary regulations in this behalf;

assess the requirements in healthcare, including human resources for health and healthcare infrastructure and develop a road map for meeting such requirements;

(c)   promote, co-ordinate and frame guidelines and lay down policies by making necessaryregulations for the proper functioning of the Commission, the Autonomous Boards and the State Medical Councils;

(d)   ensure co-ordination among the Autonomous Boards;

(e)   take such measures, as may be necessary, to ensure compliance by the State Medical Councils of the guidelines framed and regulations made under this Act for their effective functioning under thisAct;

(f)   exercise appellate jurisdiction with respect to the decisions of the Autonomous Boards;

(g)   lay down policies and codes to ensure observance of professional ethics in medical profession and to promote ethical conduct during the provision of care by medical practitioners;

(h)   frame guidelines for determination of fees and all other charges in respect of fifty per cent. of seats in private medical institutions and deemed to be universities which are governed under the provisions of this Act;

(i)   exercise such other powers and perform such other functions as may be prescribed.

(2)   All orders and decisions of the Commission shall be authenticated by the signature of theSecretary.

(3)   The Commission may delegate such of its powers of administrative and financial matters, as itdeems fit, to the Secretary.

(4)   The Commission may constitute sub-committees and delegate such of its powers to such sub-committees as may be necessary to enable them to accomplish specific tasks.

CHAPTER III - THE MEDICAL ADVISORY COUNCIL

11.   Constitution and composition of Medical Advisory Council.—(*1*) The Central Governmentshall constitute an advisory body to be known as the Medical Advisory Council.

(2)   The Council shall consist of a Chairperson and the following members, namely:—

(a)   the Chairperson of the Commission shall be the *ex officio* Chairperson of the Council;

(b)   every member of the Commission shall be the *ex officio* members of the Council;

(c)   one member to represent each State, who is the Vice-Chancellor of a health University in that State, to be nominated by that State Government;

(d)   one member to represent each Union territory, who is the Vice-Chancellor of a healthUniversity in that Union territory, to be nominated by the Ministry of Home Affairs in the Government of India;

(e)   one member to represent each State and each Union territory from amongst elected members of the State Medical Council, to be nominated by that State Medical Council;

(f)   the Chairman, University Grants Commission;

(g)   the Director, National Assessment and Accreditation Council;

(h)   four members to be nominated by the Central Government from amongst persons holding the post of Director in the Indian Institutes of Technology, Indian Institutes of Management and the Indian Institute of Science:

Provided that if there is no health University in any State or Union territory, the Vice-Chancellor of a University within that State or

Union territory having the largest number of medical colleges affiliated to it shall be nominated by the State Government or by the Ministry of Home Affairs in the Government of India:

Provided further that if there is no University in any Union territory, the Ministry of HomeAffairs shall nominate a member who possesses such medical qualification and experience as may be prescribed.

12.   Functions of Medical Advisory Council.—(*1*) The Council shall be the primary platformthrough which the States and Union territories may put forth their views and concerns before the Commission and help in shaping the overall agenda, policy and action relating to medical education and training.

(2)   The Council shall advise the Commission on measures to determine and maintain, and to co-ordinate maintenance of, the minimum standards in all matters relating to medical education, training and research.

(3)   The Council shall advise the Commission on measures to enhance equitable access to medical education.

13.   Meetings of Medical Advisory Council.—(*1*) The Council shall meet at least twice a year at such time and place as may be decided by the Chairperson.

(2)   The Chairperson shall preside at the meeting of the Council and if for any reason the Chairperson is unable to attend a meeting of the Council, such other member as nominated by the Chairperson shall preside over the meeting.

(3)   Unless the procedure is otherwise provided by regulations, fifty per cent. of the members of the Council including the Chairperson shall form the quorum and all acts of the Council shall be decided by amajority of the members present and voting.

CHAPTER IV - NATIONAL EXAMINATION

14.   **National Eligibility cum-Entrance Test.**—(*1*) There shall be a uniform National Eligibility- cum-Entrance Test for admission to the undergraduate and postgraduate super-speciality medical education in all medical institutions which are governed by the provisions of this Act:

Provided that the uniform National Eligibility-cum-Entrance Test for admission to the undergraduate medical education shall also be applicable to all medical institutions governed under any other law for the time being in force.

(2)   The Commission shall conduct the National Eligibility-cum-Entrance Test in English and in such other languages, through such designated authority and in such manner, as may be specified by regulations.

The Commission shall specify by regulations the manner of conducting common counselling by the designated authority for admission to undergraduate and postgraduate super-speciality seats in all the medical institutions which are governed by the provisions of this Act:

Provided that the designated authority of the Central Government shall conduct the common counselling for all India seats and the designated authority of the State Government shall conduct the common counselling for the seats at the State level.

15.   **National Exit Test.**—(*1*) A common final year undergraduate medical examination, to be known as the National Exit Test shall be held for granting licence to practice medicine as medical practitioners and for enrolment in the State Register or the National Register, as the case may be.

(2)   The Commission shall conduct the National Exit Test through such designated authority and in such manner as may be specified by regulations.

(3)   The National Exit Test shall become operational on such date, within three years from the date of commencement of this Act, as may be appointed by the Central Government, by notification.

(4)   Any person with a foreign medical qualification shall have to qualify National Exit Test for the purpose of obtaining licence to practice medicine as medical practitioner and for enrolment in the State Register or the National Register, as the case may be, in such manner as may be specified by regulations.

(5)   The National Exit Test shall be the basis for admission to the postgraduate broad-speciality medical education in medical institutions which are governed under the provisions of this Act or underany other law for the time being in force and shall be done in such manner as may be specified by regulations.

(6)   The Commission shall specify by regulations the manner of conducting common counselling by the designated authority for admission to the postgraduate broad-speciality seats in the medical institutions referred to in sub-section (5):

Provided that the designated authority of the Central Government shall conduct the common counselling for All India seats and the designated authority of the State Government shall conduct the common counselling for the seats at the State level.

CHAPTER V - AUTONOMOUS BOARDS

16.   Constitution of Autonomous Boards.—(1) The Central Government shall, by notification, constitute the following Autonomous Boards, under the overall supervision of the Commission, to perform the functions assigned to such Boards under this Act, namely:—

(a)   the Under-Graduate Medical Education Board;

(b)   the Post-Graduate Medical Education Board;

(c)   the Medical Assessment and Rating Board; and

(d)   the Ethics and Medical Registration Board.

(2) Each Board referred to in sub-section (1) shall be an autonomous body which shall carry out its functions under this Act subject to the regulations made by the Commission.

17.   Composition of Autonomous Boards.—(*1*) Each Autonomous Board shall consist of a Presidentand two whole-time Members and two part-time Members.

(2)   The President of each Autonomous Board, three Members (including one part-time Member) of the Under-Graduate Medical Education Board and the Post-Graduate Medical Education Board, and two Members (including one part-time Member) each of the Medical Assessment and Rating Board and the Ethics and Medical Registration Board shall be persons of outstanding ability, proven administrativecapacity and integrity, possessing a postgraduate degree in any discipline of medical sciences from any University and having experience of not less than fifteen years in such field, out of which at least seven years shall be as a leader in the area of medical education, public health, community medicine or health research.

(3)   The third Member of the Medical Assessment and Rating Board shall be a person of outstanding ability and integrity, possessing a postgraduate degree in any of the disciplines of management, quality assurance, law or science and technology from any University, having not less than fifteen years'experience in such field, out of which at least seven years shall be as a leader.

(4)   The third Member of the Ethics and Medical Registration Board shall be a person of outstanding ability who has demonstrated public record of work on medical ethics or a person of outstanding ability possessing a postgraduate degree in any of the disciplines of quality assurance, public health, law or patient advocacy from any University and having not less than fifteen years' experience in such field, out of which at least seven years shall be as a leader.

(5)   The fourth Member of each Autonomous Boards, being a part-time Member, shall be chosen fromamongst the elected Members of the State Medical Council in such manner as may be prescribed.

18.   Search Committee for appointment of President and Members.—The Central Government shall appoint the President and Members of the Autonomous Boards, except Members referred to in sub-section (*5*) of section 17, on the recommendations made by the Search Committee constituted under section 5 in accordance with the procedure specified in that section.

19.   Term of office and conditions of service of President and Members.—(*1*) The President and Members (other than part-time Members) of each Autonomous Board shall hold the office for a term not exceeding four years and shall not be eligible for any extension or re-appointment:

Provided that part-time Members of each Autonomous Board shall hold the office for a term of twoyears:

Provided further that a Member shall cease to hold office after attaining the age of seventy years.

(2)   The salaries and allowances payable to, and other terms and conditions of service of the President and Members (other than part-time Members) of an Autonomous Board shall be such as may be prescribed:

Provided that part-time Members of each Autonomous Board shall be entitled for such allowances asmay be prescribed.

(3)   The provisions of sub-sections (*3*), (*5*), (*6*), (*7*) and (*8*) of section 6 relating to other terms and conditions of service of, and section 7 relating to removal from the office of, the Chairperson and Members of the Commission shall also be applicable to the President and Members of the Autonomous Boards.

20.   Advisory committees of experts.—(*1*) Each Autonomous Board, except the Ethics and Medical Registration Board, shall be assisted by such advisory committees of experts as may be constituted by the Commission for the efficient discharge of the functions of such Boards under this Act.

(*2*) The Ethics and Medical Registration Board shall be assisted by such ethics committees of experts as may be constituted by the Commission for the efficient discharge of the functions of that Board under this Act.

Staff of Autonomous Boards.—The experts, professionals, officers and other employees appointed under section 8 shall be made available to the Autonomous Boards in such number, and in suchmanner, as may be specified by regulations by the Commission.

21.   Meetings, etc., of Autonomous Boards.—(*1*) Every Autonomous Board shall meet at least oncea month at such time and place as it may appoint.

(2)   All decisions of the Autonomous Boards shall be made by majority of votes of the President and Members.

(3)   Subject to the provision of section 28, a person who is aggrieved by any decision of an Autonomous Board may prefer an appeal to the Commission against such decision within sixty days of the communication of such decision.

22.   Powers of Autonomous Boards and delegation of powers.—(*1*) The President of each Autonomous Board shall have such administrative and financial powers as may be delegated to it by the Commission to enable such Board to function efficiently.

(*2*) The President of an Autonomous Board may further delegate any of his powers to a Member or anofficer of that Board.

23.   Powers and functions of Under-Graduate Medical Education Board.—(*1*) The Under- Graduate Medical Education Board shall perform the following functions, namely:—

(a)   determine standards of medical education at undergraduate level and oversee all aspects relating thereto;

(b)   develop competency based dynamic curriculum at undergraduate level in accordance with the regulations made under this Act;

(c)   develop competency based dynamic curriculum for addressing the needs of primary health services, community medicine and family medicine to ensure healthcare in such areas, in accordance with the provisions of the regulations made under this Act;

(d)   frame guidelines for setting up of medical institutions for imparting undergraduate courses, having regard to the needs of the country and the global norms, in accordance with the provisions of the regulations made under this Act;

(e)   determine the minimum requirements and standards for conducting courses and examinations for undergraduates in medical institutions, having regard to the needs of creativity at local levels, including designing of some courses by individual institutions, in accordance with the provisions of the regulations made under this Act;

(f)   determine standards and norms for infrastructure, faculty and quality of education in medical institutions providing undergraduate medical education in accordance with the provisions of the regulations made under this Act;

(g)   facilitate development and training of faculty members teaching undergraduate courses;

(h)   facilitate research and the international student and faculty exchange programmes relating to undergraduate medical education;

(i)   specify norms for compulsory annual disclosures, electronically or otherwise, by medical institutions, in respect of their functions that has a bearing on the interest of all stakeholders including students, faculty, the Commission and the Central Government;

(j)   grant recognition to a medical qualification at the undergraduate level.

(2) The Under-Graduate Medical Education Board may, in the discharge of its duties, make such recommendations to, and seek such directions from, the Commission, as it deems necessary.

24.   Powers and functions of Post-Graduate Medical Education Board.—(1) The Post-GraduateMedical Education Board shall perform the following functions, namely:—

(a)   determine the standards of medical education at the postgraduate level and super-speciality level in accordance with the regulations made under this Act and oversee all aspects relating thereto;

(b)   develop competency based dynamic curriculum at postgraduate level and super-speciality level in accordance with the regulations made under this Act, with a view to develop appropriate skill,knowledge, attitude, values and ethics among postgraduates and super-specialists to provide healthcare, impart medical education and conduct medical research;

(c)   frame guidelines for setting up of medical institutions for imparting postgraduate and super-speciality courses, having regard to the needs of the country and global norms, in accordance with the regulations made under this Act;

(d)   determine the minimum requirements and standards for conducting postgraduate and super-speciality courses and examinations in medical institution, in accordance with the regulations made under this Act;

(e)   determine standards and norms for infrastructure, faculty and quality of education in medical institutions conducting postgraduate and super-speciality medical education, in accordance with the regulations made under this Act;

(f)   facilitate development and training of the faculty members teaching postgraduate and super- speciality courses;

(g)   facilitate research and the international student and faculty exchange programmes relating to postgraduate and super-speciality medical education;

(h)   specify norms for compulsory annual disclosure, electronically or otherwise, by medical institutions in respect of their functions that has a bearing on the interest of all stakeholders including students, faculty, the Commission and the Central Government;

(i)   grant recognition to the medical qualifications at the postgraduate level and super-speciality level;

(j)   promote and facilitate postgraduate courses in family medicine.

(2) The Post-Graduate Medical Education Board may, in the discharge of its functions, make suchrecommendations to, and seek such directions from, the Commission, as it deems necessary.

25.   Powers and functions of Medical Assessment and Rating Board.—(1) The MedicalAssessment and Rating Board shall perform the following functions, namely:—

(a)   determine the procedure for assessing and rating the medical institutions for their compliance with the standards laid down by the Under-Graduate Medical Education Board or the Post-Graduate Medical Education Board, as the case may be, in accordance with the regulations made under this Act;

(b)   grant permission for establishment of a new medical institution, or to start any postgraduate course or to increase number of seats, in accordance with the provisions of section 28;

(c)   carry out inspections of medical institutions for assessing and rating such institutions in accordance with the regulations made under this Act:

Provided that the Medical Assessment and Rating Board may, if it deems necessary, hire and authorise

any other third party agency or persons for carrying out inspections of medical institutions for assessing and rating such institutions:

Provided further that where inspection of medical institutions is carried out by such third party agency or persons authorised by the Medical Assessment and Rating Board, it shall be obligatory on such institutions to provide access to such agency or person;

(d)   conduct, or where it deems necessary, empanel independent rating agencies to conduct, assess and rate all medical institutions, within such period of their opening, and every year thereafter, at such time, and in such manner, as may be specified by the regulations;

(e)   make available on its website or in public domain the assessment and ratings of medical institutions at regular intervals in accordance with the regulations made under this Act;

(f)   take such measures, including issuing warning, imposition of monetary penalty, reducing intake or stoppage of admissions and recommending to the Commission for withdrawal of recognition, against a medical institution for failure to maintain the minimum essential standards specified by the Under-Graduate Medical Education Board or the Post-Graduate Medical Education Board, as the case may be, in accordance with the regulations made under this Act.

(*2*) The Medical Assessment and Rating Board may, in the discharge of its functions, make such recommendations to, and seek such directions from, the Commission, as it deems necessary.

26.   Powers and functions of Ethics and Medical Registration Board.—(*1*) The Ethics and MedicalRegistration Board shall perform the following functions, namely:—

(a)   maintain National Registers of all licensed medical practitioners in accordance with the provisions of section 31;

(b)   regulate professional conduct and promote medical ethics in accordance with the regulations made under this Act:

Provided that the Ethics and Medical Registration Board shall ensure compliance of the code of professional and ethical conduct through the State Medical Council in a case where such State Medical Council has been conferred power to take disciplinary actions in respect of professional or ethical misconduct by medical practitioners under respective State Acts;

(c)   develop mechanisms to have continuous interaction with State Medical Councils to effectivelypromote and regulate the conduct of medical practitioners and professionals;

(d)   exercise appellate jurisdiction with respect to the actions taken by a State Medical Council under section 30.

(*2*) The Ethics and Medical Registration Board may, in the discharge of its duties, make suchrecommendations to, and seek such directions from, the Commission, as it deems necessary.

27.   Permission for establishment of new medical college.— (*1*) No person shall establish a new medical college or start any postgraduate course or increase number of seats without obtaining prior permission of the Medical Assessment and Rating Board.

(2)   For the purposes of obtaining permission under sub-section (*1*), a person may submit a scheme to the Medical Assessment and Rating Board in such form, containing such particulars, accompanied bysuch fee, and in such manner, as may be specified by the regulations.

(3)   The Medical Assessment and Rating Board shall, having due

regard to the criteria specified in section 29, consider the scheme received under sub-section (2) and either approve or disapprove such scheme within a period of six months from the date of such receipt:

Provided that before disapproving such scheme, an opportunity to rectify the defects, if any, shall begiven to the person concerned.

(4)   Where a scheme is approved under sub-section (3), such approval shall be the permission under sub-section (1) to establish new medical college.

(5)   Where a scheme is disapproved under sub-section (3), or where no decision is taken within six months of submitting a scheme under sub-section (1), the person concerned may prefer an appeal to the Commission for approval of the scheme within fifteen days of such disapproval or, as the case may be, lapse of six months, in such manner as may be specified by the regulations.

(6)   The Commission shall decide the appeal received under sub-section (5) within a period of forty-five days from the date of receipt of the appeal and in case the Commission approves the scheme, such approval shall be the permission under sub-section (1) to establish a new medical college and in case the Commission disapproves the scheme, or fails to give its decision within the specified period, the person concerned may prefer a second appeal to the Central Government within thirty days of communication of such disapproval or, as the case may be, lapse of specified period.

(7)   The Medical Assessment and Rating Board may conduct evaluation and assessment of any medical institution at any time, either directly or through any other expert having integrity and experienceof medical profession and without any prior notice and assess and evaluate the performance, standardsand benchmarks of such medical institution.

Explanation.—For the purposes of this section, the term "person" includes a University, trust or anyother association of persons or body of individuals, but does not include the Central Government.

28.   Criteria for approving or disapproving scheme.—While approving or disapproving a scheme under section 28, the Medical

Assessment and Rating Board, or the Commission, as the case may be,shall take into consideration the following criteria, namely:—

(a)   adequacy of financial resources;

(b)   whether adequate academic faculty and other necessary facilities have been provided toensure proper functioning of medical college or would be provided within the time-limit specified in the scheme;

(c)   whether adequate hospital facilities have been provided or would be provided within the time-limit specified in the scheme;

(d)   such other factors as may be prescribed:

Provided that, subject to the previous approval of the Central Government, the criteria may be relaxed for the medical colleges which are set up in such areas as may be specified by the regulations.

29.   State Medical Councils.—(*1*) The State Government shall, within three years of the commencement of this Act, take necessary steps to establish a State Medical Council if no such Council exists in that State.

(2)   Where a State Act confers power upon the State Medical Council to take disciplinary actions in respect of any professional or ethical misconduct by a registered medical practitioner or professional, the State Medical Council shall act in accordance with the regulations made, and the guidelines framed, underthis Act:

Provided that till such time as a State Medical Council is established in a State, the Ethics andMedical Registration Board shall receive the complaints and grievances relating to any professional or ethical misconduct against a registered medical practitioner or professional in that State in accordance with such procedure as may be specified by the regulations:

Provided further that the Ethics and Medical Registration Board or, as the case may be, the State Medical Council shall give an opportunity of hearing to the medical practitioner or professional concerned before taking any action, including imposition of any monetary penalty against such person.

(3)	A medical practitioner or professional who is aggrieved by any action taken by a State Medical Council under sub-section (2) may prefer an appeal to the Ethics and Medical Registration Board against such action, and the decision, if any, of the Ethics and Medical Registration Board thereupon shall be binding on the State Medical Council, unless a second appeal is preferred under sub-section (4).

(4)	A medical practitioner or professional who is aggrieved by the decision of the Ethics and Medical Registration Board may prefer an appeal to the Commission within sixty days of communication of such decision.

Explanation.—For the purposes of this Act,—

(a)	"State" includes Union territory and the expressions "State Government" and "State Medical Council", in relation to a Union territory, shall respectively mean the "Central Government" and "Union territory Medical Council";

(b)	the expression "professional or ethical misconduct" includes any act of commission or omission as may be specified by the regulations.

**30.	National Register and State Register.**—(1) The Ethics and Medical Registration Board shall maintain a National Register containing the name, address, all recognised qualifications possessed by a licensed medical practitioner and such other particulars as may be specified by the regulations.

(2)	The National Register shall be maintained in such form, including electronic form, in such manner, as may be specified by the regulations.

(3)	The manner in which a name or qualification may be added to, or removed from, the National Register and the grounds for removal thereof, shall be such as may be specified by the regulations.

(4)	The National Register shall be a public document within the meaning of section 74 of the Indian Evidence Act, 1872 (1 of 1872).

(5)	The National Register shall be made available to the public by placing it on the website of the Ethics and Medical Registration Board.

(6)   Every State Medical Council shall maintain and regularly update the State Register in thespecified electronic format and supply a physical copy of the same to the Ethics and Medical Registration Board within three months of the commencement of this Act.

(7)   The Ethics and Medical Registration Board shall ensure electronic synchronisation of the National Register and the State Register in such a manner that any change in one register is automatically reflected in the other register.

(8)   The Ethics and Medical Registration Board shall maintain a separate National Register in such form, containing such particulars, including the name, address and all recognised qualifications possessed by a Community Health Provider referred to in section 32 in such manner as may be specified by the regulations.

31.   Community Health Provider.—(*1*) The Commission may grant limited licence to practice medicine at mid-level as Community Health Provider to such person connected with modern scientific medical profession who qualify such criteria as may be specified by the regulations:

Provided that the number of limited licence to be granted under this sub-section shall not exceed one-third of the total number of licenced medical practitioners registered under sub-section (*1*) of section 31.

(2)   The Community Health Provider who is granted limited licences under sub-section (*1*), may practice medicine to such extent, in such circumstances and for such period, as may be specified by the regulations.

(3)   The Community Health Provider may prescribe specified medicine independently, only in primaryand preventive healthcare, but in cases other than primary and preventive healthcare, he may prescribe medicine only under the supervision of medical practitioners registered under sub-section (*1*) of section 31.

32. **Rights of persons to have licence to practice and to be enrolled in National Register or State Register and their obligations thereto.**—(*1*) Any person who qualifies the National Exit Test held under section 15 shall be granted a licence to practice medicine and shall have his name and qualifications enrolled in the National Register or a State Register, as the case may be:

Provided that a person who has been registered in the Indian Medical Register maintained under the Indian Medical Council Act, 1956 (102 of 1956) prior to the coming into force of this Act and before the National Exit Test becomes operational under sub-section (*3*) of section 15, shall be deemed to have been registered under this Act and be enrolled in the National Register maintained under this Act.

(2) No person who has obtained medical qualification from a medical institution established in any country outside India and is recognised as a medical practitioner in that country, shall, after the commencement of this Act and the National Exit Test becomes operational under sub-section (*3*) of section 15, be enrolled in the National Register unless he qualifies the National Exit Test.

(3) When a person whose name is entered in the State Register or the National Register, as the case may be, obtains any title, diploma or other qualification for proficiency in sciences or public health or medicine which is a recognised medical qualification under section 35 or section 36, as the case may be, he shall be entitled to have such title, diploma or qualification entered against his name in the State Register or the National Register, as the case may be, in such manner as may be specified by the regulations.

33. **Bar to practice.**—(*1*) No person other than a person who is enrolled in the State Register or the National Register, as the case may be, shall—

(a) be allowed to practice medicine as a qualified medical practitioner;

(b) hold office as a physician or surgeon or any other office, by whatever name called, which is meant to be held by a physician or surgeon;

(c)   be entitled to sign or authenticate a medical or fitness certificate or any other certificaterequired by any law to be signed or authenticated by a duly qualified medical practitioner;

(d)   be entitled to give evidence at any inquest or in any court of law as an expert under section 45of the Indian Evidence Act, 1872 (1 of 1872) on any matter relating to medicine:

Provided that the Commission shall submit a list of such medical professionals to the CentralGovernment in such manner as may be prescribed:

Provided further that a foreign citizen who is enrolled in his country as a medical practitioner in accordance with the law regulating the registration of medical practitioners in that country may be permitted temporary registration in India for such period and in such manner as may be specified by the regulations.

(2) Any person who contravenes any of the provisions of this section shall be punished with imprisonment for a term which may extend to one year, or with fine which may extend to five lakh rupeesor with both.

CHAPTER VI - RECOGNITION OF MEDICAL QUALIFICATIONS

34.   Recognition of medical qualifications granted by Universities or medical institutions in India.—(*1*) The medical qualification granted by any University or medical institution in India shall be listed and maintained by the Under-Graduate Medical Education Board or the Post-Graduate Medical Education Board, as the case may be, in such manner as may be specified by the regulations and such medical qualification shall be a recognised medical qualification for the purposes of this Act.

(2)   Any University or medical institution in India which grants an undergraduate or postgraduate or super-speciality medical qualification not included in the list maintained by the Under-Graduate Medical Education Board or the Post-Graduate Medical Education Board, as the case may be, may apply to that Board for granting recognition to such qualification.

(3)   The Under-Graduate Medical Education Board or the Post-Graduate Medical Education Board, as the case may be, shall examine the application for grant of recognition to a medical qualification within a period of six months in such manner as may be specified by the regulations.

(4)   Where the Under-Graduate Medical Education Board or the Post-Graduate Medical Education Board, as the case may be, decides to grant recognition to a medical qualification, it shall include such medical qualification in the list maintained by it and also specify the date of effect of such recognition.

(5)   Where the Under-Graduate Medical Education Board or the Post-Graduate Medical Education Board, as the case may be, decides not to grant recognition to a medical qualification, the University or the medical institution concerned may prefer an appeal to the Commission for grant of recognition within sixty days of the communication of such decision, in such manner as may be specified by the regulations.

(6)   The Commission shall examine the appeal received under sub-section (5) within a period of two months and if it decides that recognition may be granted to such medical qualification, it may direct the Under-Graduate Medical Education Board or the Post-Graduate Medical Education Board, as the case may be, to include such medical qualification in the list maintained by that Board, in such manner as may be specified by the regulations.

(7)   Where the Commission decides not to grant recognition to the medical qualification, or fails to take a decision within the specified period, the University or the medical institution concerned may prefer a second appeal to the Central Government within thirty days of the communication of such decision or lapse of specified period, as the case may be.

(8)   All medical qualifications which have been recognised before the date of commencement of this Act and are included in the First Schedule and Part I of the Third Schedule to the Indian Medical Council Act, 1956 (102 of 1956), shall also be recognised medical qualifications for the purposes of this Act, and shall be listed and maintained by the Under-Graduate Medical Education Board or the

Post-Graduate Medical Education Board, as the case may be, in such manner as may be specified by the regulations.

35.   Recognition of medical qualifications granted by medical institutions outside India.—(*1*) Where an authority in any country outside India, which by the law of that country is entrusted with the recognition of medical qualifications in that country, makes an application to the Commission for granting recognition to such medical qualification in India, the Commission may, subject to such verification as it may deem necessary, either grant or refuse to grant recognition to that medical qualification:

Provided that the Commission shall give a reasonable opportunity of being heard to such authority before refusing to grant such recognition.

(2)   A medical qualification which is granted recognition by the Commission under sub-section (*1*) shall be a recognised medical qualification for the purposes of this Act, and such qualification shall be listed and maintained by the Commission in such manner as may be specified by the regulations.

(3)   Where the Commission refuses to grant recognition to the medical qualification under sub-section (*1*), the authority concerned may prefer an appeal to the Central Government against such decision within thirty days of communication thereof.

(4)   All medical qualifications which have been recognised before the date of commencement of this Act and are included in the Second Schedule and Part II of the Third Schedule to the Indian Medical Council Act, 1956 (102 of 1956), shall also be recognised medical qualifications for the purposes of this Act, and shall be listed and maintained by the Commission in such manner as may be specified by the regulations.

36.   Recognition of medical qualifications granted by statutory or other body in India.—(*1*) The medical qualifications granted by any statutory or other body in India which are covered by the categories listed in the Schedule shall be recognised medical qualifications for the purposes of this Act.

(2)   The Diplomate of National Board in broad-speciality qualifications and superspeciality qualifications when granted in a medical institution with attached hospital or in a hospital with the strength of five hundred or more beds, by the National Board of Examinations, shall be equivalent in all respects to the corresponding postgraduate qualification and the super-speciality qualification granted under this Act, but in all other cases, senior residency in a medical college for an additional period of one year shall be required for such qualification to be equivalent for the purposes of teaching also.

(3)   The Central Government may, on the recommendation of the Commission, and having regard to the objects of this Act, by notification, add to, or, as the case may be, omit from, the Schedule any categories of medical qualifications granted by a statutory or other body in India and on such addition, or as the case may be, omission, the medical qualifications granted by such statutory or other body in India shall be, or shall cease to be, recognised medical qualifications for the purposes of this Act.

37.   Withdrawal of recognition granted to medical qualification granted by medical institutions in India.—(*1*) Where, upon receiving a report from the Medical Assessment and Rating Board under section 26, or otherwise, if the Commission is of the opinion that—

(a)   the courses of study and examination to be undergone in, or the proficiency required from candidates at any examination held by, a University or medical institution do not conform to the standards specified by the Under-Graduate Medical Education Board or the Post-Graduate Medical Education Board, as the case may be; or

(b)   the standards and norms for infrastructure, faculty and quality of education in medicalinstitution as determined by the Under-Graduate Medical Education Board or the Post-Graduate Medical Education Board, as the case may be, are not adhered to by any University or medical institution, and such University or medical institution has failed to take necessary corrective action to maintain specified minimum standards, the Commission may initiate action in accordance with theprovisions of sub-section (2):

Provided that the Commission shall, before taking any action for *suo motu* withdrawal of recognition granted to the medical qualification awarded by a University or medical institution, impose penalty in accordance with the provisions of clause (f) of sub-section (1) of section 26.

(2) The Commission shall, after making such further inquiry as it deems fit, and after holding consultations with the concerned State Government and the authority of the concerned University or medical institution, comes to the conclusion that the recognition granted to a medical qualification ought to be withdrawn, it may, by order, withdraw recognition granted to such medical qualification and direct the Under-Graduate Medical Education Board or the Post-Graduate Medical Education Board, as the casemay be, to amend the entries against the University or medical institution concerned in the list maintainedby that Board to the effect that the recognition granted to such medical qualification is withdrawn with effect from the date specified in that order.

38.   Derecognition of medical qualifications granted by medical institutions outside India.— Where, after verification with the authority in any country outside India, the Commission is of the opinionthat a recognised medical qualification which is included in the list maintained by it is to be derecognised,it may, by order, derecognise such medical qualification and remove it from the list maintained by the Commission with effect from the date of such order.

39.   Special provision in certain cases for recognition of medical qualifications.—Where the Commission deems it necessary, it may, by an order published in the Official Gazette, direct that any medical qualification granted by a medical institution in a country outside India, after such date as may bespecified in that notification, shall be a recognised medical qualification for the purposes of this Act:

Provided   that   medical   practice   by   a   person   possessing   such qualification shall be permitted only if such person qualifies National Exit Test.

CHAPTER VII - GRANTS, AUDIT AND ACCOUNTS

40. Grants by Central Government.—The Central Government may, after due appropriation made by Parliament by law in this behalf, make to the Commission grants of such sums of money as the CentralGovernment may think fit.

41. National Medical Commission Fund.—(*1*) There shall be constituted a fund to be called "the National Medical Commission Fund" which shall form part of the public account of India and there shall be credited thereto—

(a)   all Government grants, fees, penalties and charges received by the Commission and the Autonomous Boards;

(b)   all sums received by the Commission from such other sources as may be decided by it.

(2)   The Fund shall be applied for making payment towards—

(a)   the salaries and allowances payable to the Chairperson and Members of the Commission, the Presidents and Members of the Autonomous Boards and the administrative expenses including the salaries and allowances payable to the officers and other employees of the Commission and Autonomous Boards;

(b)   the expenses incurred in carrying out the provisions of this Act, including in connection with the discharge of the functions of the Commission and the Autonomous Boards.

42. Audit and accounts.—(*1*) The Commission shall maintain proper accounts and other relevant records and prepare an annual statement of accounts in such form as may be prescribed, in consultation with the Comptroller and Auditor-General of India.

(2)   The accounts of the Commission shall be audited by the Comptroller and Auditor-General of Indiaat such intervals as may be

specified by him and any expenditure incurred in connection with such audit shall be payable by the Commission to the Comptroller and Auditor-General of India.

(3)   The Comptroller and Auditor-General of India and any other persons appointed by him in connection with the audit of the accounts of the Commission shall have the same rights and privileges and authority in connection with such audit as the Comptroller and Auditor-General generally has in connection with the audit of Government accounts and in particular, shall have the right to demand the production of, and complete access to, records, books, accounts, connected vouchers and other documentsand papers and to inspect the office of the Commission.

(4)   The accounts of the Commission as certified by the Comptroller and Auditor-General of India or any other person appointed by him in this behalf, together with the audit report thereon, shall be forwarded annually by the Commission to the Central Government which shall cause the same to be laid, as soon as may be after it is received, before each House of Parliament.

43.   Furnishing of returns and reports to Central Government.—(*1*) The Commission shall furnish to the Central Government, at such time, in such form and in such manner, as may be prescribedor as the Central Government may direct, such reports and statements, containing such particulars in regard to any matter under the jurisdiction of the Commission, as the Central Government may, from timeto time, require.

(2)   The Commission shall prepare, once every year, in such form and at such time as may be prescribed, an annual report, giving a summary of its activities during the previous year and copies of the report shall be forwarded to the Central Government.

(3)   A copy of the report received under sub-section (*2*) shall be laid by the Central Government, as soon as may be after it is received, before each House of Parliament.

CHAPTER VIII - MISCELLANEOUS

44. Power of Central Government to give directions to Commission and Autonomous Boards.—

(1) Without prejudice to the foregoing provisions of this Act, the Commission and the Autonomous Boards shall, in exercise of their powers and discharge of their functions under this Act, be bound by such directions on questions of policy as the Central Government may give in writing to them from time to time:

Provided that the Commission and the Autonomous Boards shall, as far as practicable, be given an opportunity to express their views before any direction is given under this sub-section.

(2) The decision of the Central Government whether a question is one of policy or not shall be final.

45. Power of Central Government to give directions to State Governments.—

The Central Government may give such directions, as it may deem necessary, to a State Government for carrying out all or any of the provisions of this Act and the State Government shall comply with such directions.

46. Information to be furnished by Commission and publication thereof.—

(1) The Commission shall furnish such reports, copies of its minutes, abstracts of its accounts, and other information to the Central Government as that Government may require.

(2) The Central Government may publish, in such manner as it may think fit, the reports, minutes, abstracts of accounts and other information furnished to it under sub-section (1)

47. Obligation of universities and medical institutions.—

Every University and medical institution governed under this Act shall maintain a website at all times and display on its website all such information as may be required by the Commission or an Autonomous Board, as the case may be.

48.   Completion of courses of studies in medical institutions.—(*1*) Notwithstanding anything contained in this Act, any student who was studying for a degree, diploma or certificate in any medical institution immediately before the commencement of this Act shall continue to so study and complete his course for such degree, diploma or certificate, and such institution shall continue to provide instructions and examination for such student in accordance with the syllabus and studies as existed before such commencement, and such student shall be deemed to have completed his course of study under this Act and shall be awarded degree, diploma or certificate under this Act.

(*2*) Notwithstanding anything contained in this Act, where recognition granted to a medical institutionhas lapsed, whether by efflux of time or by its voluntary surrender or for any other reason whatsoever, such medical institution shall continue to maintain and provide the minimum standards required to be provided under this Act till such time as all candidates who are admitted in that medical institution complete their study.

49.   Joint sittings of Commission, Central Councils of Homoeopathy and Indian medicine to enhance interface between their respective systems of medicine.—(*1*) There shall be a joint sitting of the Commission, the Central Council of Homoeopathy and the Central Council of Indian Medicine atleast once a year, at such time and place as they mutually appoint, to enhance the interface between Homoeopathy, Indian Systems of Medicine and modern systems of medicine.

(2)   The agenda for the joint sitting may be prepared with mutual agreement between the Chairpersonsof the Commission, the Central Council of Homoeopathy and the Central Council of Indian Medicine or be prepared separately by each of them.

(3)   The joint sitting referred to in sub-section (*1*) may, by an affirmative vote of all members present and voting, decide on approving specific educational modules or programmes that may be introduced in the undergraduate course and the postgraduate course across medical systems and promote medical pluralism.

50.   State Government to promote primary healthcare in rural areas.—Every State Government may, for the purposes of addressing or promoting primary healthcare in rural area, take necessarymeasures to enhance the capacity of the healthcare professionals.

51.   Chairperson, Members, officers of Commission and of Autonomous Boards to be public servants.—The Chairperson, Members, officers and other employees of the Commission and the President, Members and officers and other employees of the Autonomous Boards shall be deemed, when acting or purporting to act in pursuance of any of the provisions of this Act, to be public servants within the meaning of section 21 of the Indian Penal Code 1860 (45 of 1860).

52.   Protection of action taken in good faith.—No suit, prosecution or other legal proceeding shall lie against the Government, the Commission or any Autonomous Board or a State Medical Council or anyCommittee thereof, or any officer or other employee of the Government or of the Commission acting under this Act for anything which is in good faith done or intended to be done under this Act or the rules or regulations made thereunder.

53.   Cognizance of offences.—No court shall take cognizance of an offence punishable under this Act except upon a complaint in writing made in this behalf by an officer authorised by the Commission or the Ethics and Medical Registration Board or a State Medical Council, as the case may be.

54.   Power of Central Government to supersede Commission.—(*1*) If, at any time, the Central Government is of opinion that—

(a)   the Commission is unable to discharge the functions and duties imposed on it by or under the provisions of this Act; or

(b)   the Commission has persistently made default in complying with any direction issued by the Central Government under this Act or in the discharge of the functions and duties imposed on it by orunder the provisions of this Act, the Central Government may, by notification, supersede the Commission for such period, not exceedingsix months, as may be specified in the notification:

Provided that before issuing a notification under this sub-section, the Central Government shall give a reasonable opportunity to the Commission to show cause as to why it should not be superseded and shall consider the explanations and objections, if any, of the Commission.

(2)   Upon the publication of a notification under sub-section (*1*) superseding the Commission,—

(a)   all the Members shall, as from the date of supersession, vacate their offices as such;

(b)   all the powers, functions and duties which may, by or under the provisions of this Act, be exercised or discharged by or on behalf of the Commission, shall, until the Commission is re-constituted under sub-section (*3*), be exercised and discharged by such person or persons as the Central Government may direct;

(c)   all property owned or controlled by the Commission shall, until the Commission is re-constituted under sub-section (*3*), vest in the Central Government.

(3)   On the expiration of the period of supersession specified in the notification issued under sub-section (*1*), the Central Government may,—

(a)   extend the period of supersession for such further term not exceeding six months, as it may consider necessary; or

(b)   re-constitute the Commission by fresh appointment and in such case the Members who vacated their offices under clause (*a*) of sub-section (*2*) shall not be deemed disqualified for appointment:

Provided that the Central Government may, at any time before the expiration of the period of supersession, whether as originally specified under sub-section (*1*) or as extended under this sub-section, take action under clause (*b*) of this sub-section.

(4)   The Central Government shall cause a notification issued under sub-section (*1*) and a full report of any action taken under this section and the circumstances leading to such action to be laid before both Houses of Parliament at the earliest opportunity.

55.   Power to make rules.—(*1*) The Central Government may, by notification, make rules to carryout the purposes of this Act.

(2)   In particular, and without prejudice to the generality of the foregoing power, such rules may provide for all or any of the following matters, namely:—

(a)   the manner of appointing ten Members of the Commission on rotational basis from amongst the nominees of the States and Union territories in the Medical Advisory Council under clause (*b*) of sub-section (*4*) of section 4;

(b)   the manner of appointing nine members of the Commission under clause (*c*) of sub-section (*4*)of section 4;

(c)   the manner of nominating one expert by the Central Government under clause (*c*) of sub-section (*1*) of section 5;

(d)   the salary and allowances payable to, and other terms and conditions of service of the Chairperson and Members under sub-section (*4*) of section 6;

(e)   the form and the manner of making declaration under sub-section (*6*) of section 6;

(f)   the qualifications and experience to be possessed by the Secretary of the Commission under sub-section (*2*) of section 8;

(g)   the salaries and allowances payable to, and other terms and conditions of service of the Secretary, officers and other employees of the Commission under sub-section (*6*) of section 8;

(h)   the other powers and functions of the Commission under clause (*j*) of sub-section (*1*) of section 10;

(i)   the medical qualification and experience to be possessed by a member under the second proviso to section 11;

(j)   the manner of choosing part-time Members under sub-section (*5*) of section 17;

(k)   the salary and allowances payable to, and other terms and conditions of service of the President and Members of an Autonomous Board under sub-section (*2*), and the allowances payable to part-time Members under the proviso thereunder, of section 19;

(l)   the other factors under clause (*d*) of section 29;

(m)   the manner of submitting a list of medical professionals under the first proviso to sub-section (*1*) of section 34;

(n)   the form for preparing annual statement of accounts under sub-section (*1*) of section 43;

(o)   the time within which, and the form and the manner in which, the reports and statements shall be furnished by the Commission and the particulars with regard to any matter as may be required by the Central Government under sub-section (*1*) of section 44;

(p)   the form and the time for preparing annual report under sub-section (*2*) of section 44;

(q)   any other matter in respect of which provision is to be made by rules.

56.   Power to make regulations.—(*1*) The Commission may, after previous publication, by notification, make regulations consistent with this Act and the rules made thereunder to carry out the provisions of this Act.

(2)   In particular, and without prejudice to the generality of the foregoing power, such regulations mayprovide for all or any of the following matters, namely:—

(a)   the functions to be discharged by the Secretary of the Commission under sub-section (*4*) of section 8;

(b)   the procedure in accordance with which experts and professionals may be engaged and the number of such experts and professionals under sub-section (*7*) of section 8;

(c)   the procedure to be followed at the meetings of Commission, including the quorum at its meetings under sub-section (*3*) of section 9;

(d)   the quality and standards to be maintained in medical education under clause (*a*) of sub-section (*1*) of section 10;

(e)   the manner of regulating medical institutions, medical researches and medical professionals under clause (*b*) of sub-section (*1*) of section 10;

(f)　　　　the manner of functioning of the Commission, the Autonomous Boards and the State Medical Councils under clause (*d*) of sub-section (*1*) of section 10;

(g)　　　　the procedure to be followed at the meetings of the Medical Advisory Council, including the quorum at its meetings under sub-section (*3*) of section 13;

(h)　　　　the other languages in which and the manner in which the National Eligibility-cum-Entrance Test shall be conducted under sub-section (*2*) of section 14;

(i)　　　　the manner of conducting common counselling by the designated authority for admission to the undergraduate and postgraduate super-speciality medical education under sub-section (*3*) ofsection 14;

(j)　　　　the designated authority, and the manner for conducting the National Exit Test under sub-section (*2*) of section 15;

(k)　　　　the manner in which a person with foreign medical qualification shall qualify National Exit Test under sub-section (*4*) of section 15;

(l)　　　　the manner in which admission to the postgraduate broad-speciality medical education shall bemade on the basis of National Exit Test under sub-section (*5*) of section 15;

(m)　　　　the manner of conducting common counselling by the designated authority for admission to the postgraduate broad-speciality medical education under sub-section (*6*) of section 15;

(n)　　　　the number of, and the manner in which, the experts, professionals, officers and otheremployees shall be made available by the Commission to the Autonomous Boards under section 21;

(o)　　　　the curriculum at undergraduate level under clause (*b*) of sub-section (*1*) of section 24;

(p)　　　　the curriculum for primary medicine, community medicine and family medicine under clause

(c)　　of sub-section (*1*) of section 24;

(q)　　　　the manner of imparting undergraduate courses by

medical institutions under clause (*d*) of sub-section (*1*) of section 24;

(r)	the minimum requirements and standards for conducting courses and examinations for undergraduates in medical institutions under clause (*e*) of sub-section (*1*) of section 24;

(s)	the standards and norms for infrastructure, faculty and quality of education at undergraduate level in medical institutions under clause (*f*) of sub-section (*1*) of section 24;

(t)	the standards of medical education at the postgraduate level and superspeciality level under clause (*a*) of sub-section (*1*) of section 25;

(u)	the curriculum at postgraduate level and super-speciality level under clause (*b*) of sub-section (*1*) of section 25;

(v)	the manner of imparting postgraduate and super-speciality courses by medical institutions under clause (*c*) of sub-section (*1*) of section 25;

(w)	the minimum requirements and standards for conducting postgraduate and super-speciality courses and examinations in medical institutions under clause (*d*) of sub-section (*1*) of section 25;

(x)	the standards and norms for infrastructure, faculty and quality of education in medicalinstitutions conducting postgraduate and super-speciality medical education under clause (*e*) of sub-section (*1*) of section 25;

(y)	the procedure for assessing and rating the medical institutions under clause (*a*) of sub-section (*1*) of section 26;

(z)	the manner of carrying out inspections of medical institutions for assessing and rating such institutions under clause (*c*) of sub-section (*1*) of section 26;

(*za*) the manner of conducting, and the manner of empanelling independent rating agencies to conduct, assessment and rating of medical institutions under clause (*d*) of sub-section (*1*) of section 26;

(*zb*) the manner of making available on website or in public domain the assessment and ratings of medical institutions under clause (*e*) of sub-section (*1*) of section 26;

(*zc*) the measures to be taken against a medical institution for its failure to maintain the minimum essential standards under clause (*f*) of sub-section (*1*) of section 26;

(*zd*) the manner of regulating professional conduct and promoting medical ethics under clause (*b*) of sub-section (*1*) of section 27;

(*ze*) the form of scheme, the particulars thereof, the fee to be accompanied and the manner of submitting scheme for establishing a new medical college or for starting any postgraduate course or for increasing number of seats under sub-section (*2*) of section 28;

(*zf*) the manner of making an appeal to the Commission for approval of the scheme under sub-section (*5*) of section 28;

(*zg*) the areas in respect of which criteria may be relaxed under the proviso to section 29;

(*zh*) the manner of taking disciplinary action by a State Medical Council for professional orethical misconduct of registered medical practitioner or professional and the procedure for receiving complaints and grievances by Ethics and Medical Registration Board, under sub-section (*2*) of section 30;

(*zi*) the act of commission or omission which amounts to professional or ethical misconduct underclause (*b*) of the Explanation to section 30;

(*zj*) other particulars to be contained in a National Register under sub-section (*1*) of section 31;

(*zk*) the form, including the electronic form and the manner of maintaining the National Registerunder sub-section (*2*) of section 31;

(*zl*) the manner in which any name or qualification may be added to, or removed from, theNational Register and the grounds for removal thereof, under sub-section (*3*) of section 31;

(*zm*) the form and manner in which the National Register for registering Community HealthProvider is to be maintained under sub-section (*8*) of section 31;

(*zn*) the criteria for granting limited licence to practice medicine under sub-section (*1*) of section

32;

(*zo*) the extent, the circumstances and the period under sub-section (*2*) of section 32;

(*zp*) the manner of listing and maintaining medical qualifications granted by a University or

medical institution in India under sub-section (*1*) of section 35;

(*zq*) the manner of examining the application for grant of recognition under sub-section (*3*) of section 35;

(*zr*) the manner of preferring an appeal to the Commission for grant of recognition undersub-section (*5*) of section 35;

(*zs*) the manner of including a medical qualification in the list maintained by the Board undersub-section (*6*) of section 35;

(*zt*) the manner of listing and maintaining medical qualifications which have been granted recognition before the date of commencement of this Act under sub-section (*8*) of section 35.

57.   Rules and regulations to be laid before Parliament.— Every rule and every regulation made, and every notification issued, under this Act shall be laid, as soon as may be after it is made, before each House of Parliament, while it is in session, for a total period of thirty days which may be comprised inone session or in two or more successive sessions, and if, before the expiry of the session immediately following the session or the successive sessions aforesaid, both Houses agree in making any modification in the rule or regulation or notification; both Houses agree that the rule or regulation or notificationshould not be made, the rule or regulation or notification shall thereafter have effect only in such modifiedform or be of no effect, as the case may be; so, however, that any such modification or annulment shall be without prejudice to the validity of anything previously done under that rule or regulation or notification.

58.   Power to remove difficulties.—(*1*) If any difficulty arises in giving effect to the provisions ofthis Act, the Central Government may, by order published in the Official Gazette, make such provisions not inconsistent with the provisions of this Act, as may appear to it to be necessary, for removing the difficulty:

Provided that no order shall be made under this section after the expiry of a period of two years fromthe commencement of this Act.

(2) Every order made under this section shall be laid, as soon as may be after it is made, before each House of Parliament.

59.   Repeal and saving.—(1) With effect from such date as the Central Government may appoint in this behalf, the Indian Medical Council Act, 1956 (102 of 1956) shall stand repealed and the Medical Council of India constituted under sub-section (1) of section 3 of the said Act shall stand dissolved.

(2)   Notwithstanding the repeal of the Act referred to in sub-section (1), it shall not affect,—

(a)   the previous operation of the Act so repealed or anything duly done or suffered thereunder; or

(b)   any right, privilege, obligation or liability acquired, accrued or incurred under the Act so repealed; or

(c)   any penalty incurred in respect of any contravention under the Act so repealed; or

(d)   any proceeding or remedy in respect of any such right, privilege, obligation, liability, penalty as aforesaid, and any such proceeding or remedy may be instituted, continued or enforced, and any such penalty may be imposed as if that Act had not been repealed.

(3)   On the dissolution of the Medical Council of India, the person appointed as the Chairman of the Medical Council of India and every other person appointed as the Member and any officer and other employee of that Council and holding office as such immediately before such dissolution shall vacate their respective offices and such Chairman and other Members shall be entitled to claim compensation notexceeding three months' pay and allowances for the premature termination of term of their office or of any contract of service:

Provided that any officer or other employee who has been, immediately before the dissolution of the Medical Council of India appointed on deputation basis to the Medical Council of India, shall, on such dissolution, stand reverted to his parent cadre, Ministry or Department, as the case may be:

Provided further that any officer or other employee who has been, immediately before the dissolution of the Medical Council of India, employed on regular or contractual basis by the Medical Council of India, shall, on and from such dissolution, cease to be the officer or employee of the Medical Council of India and his employment in the Medical Council of India stand terminated with immediate effect:

Provided also that such officer or employee of the Medical Council of India shall be entitled to such compensation for the premature termination of his employment, which shall not be less than three months'pay and allowances, as may be prescribed.

(4)   Notwithstanding the repeal of the aforesaid enactment, any order made, any licence to practice issued, any registration made, any permission to start new medical college or to start higher course of studies or for increase in the admission capacity granted, any recognition of medical qualifications granted, under the Indian Medical Council Act, 1956 (102 of 1956), which are in force as on the date of commencement of this Act, shall continue to be in force till the date of their expiry for all purposes, as if they had been issued or granted under the provisions of this Act or the rules or regulations made thereunder.

60.   Transitory provisions.—(*1*) The Commission shall be the successor in interest to the Medical Council of India including its subsidiaries or owned trusts and all the assets and liabilities of the Medical Council of India shall be deemed to have been transferred to the Commission.

(2)   Notwithstanding the repeal of the Indian Medical Council Act, 1956 (102 of 1956), the educational standards, requirements and other provisions of the Indian Medical Council Act, 1956 and therules and regulations made thereunder shall continue to be in force and operate till new standards or requirements are specified under this Act or the rules and regulations made thereunder:

Provided that anything done or any action taken as regards the educational standards and requirements under the enactment under repeal and the rules and regulations made thereunder shall be deemed to have been done or taken under the corresponding provisions of this

Act and shall continue in force accordingly unless and until superseded by anything done or by any action taken under this Act.

THE SCHEDULE

[*See* section 37]

LIST OF CATEGORIES OF MEDICAL QUALIFICATIONS GRANTED BY STATUTORY BODY OR OTHER BODY IN INDIA

Sl. No.   *Categories of medical qualifications*

1.   All medical qualifications granted by the Jawaharlal Institute of Postgraduate Medical Education and Research, Puducherry.

2.   All medical qualifications granted by All India Institutes of Medical Sciences.

3.   All medical qualifications granted by the Postgraduate Institute of Medical Education andResearch, Chandigarh.

4.   All medical qualifications granted by the National Institute of Mental Health and Neuro-Sciences, Bangalore.

All medical qualifications granted by the National Board of Examination

Clinical Establishments (Registration and Regulation) Act, 2010.

SECTIONS

CHAPTER I - PRELIMINARY

CHAPTER II - THE NATIONAL COUNCIL FOR CLINICAL ESTABLISHMENTS

CHAPTER III - REGISTRATION AND STANDARDS FOR CLINICAL ESTABLISHMENTS

CHAPTER IV - PROCEDURE FOR REGISTRATION

SECTIONS

CHAPTERV - REGISTER OF CLINICAL ESTABLISHMENTS

CHAPTERVI - PENALTIES

Penalty.

CHAPTER VII - MISCELLANEOUS

The Clinical Establishments (Registration and Regulation) Act, 2010

ACT NO. 23 OF 2010

18*th August*, 2010.]

An Act to provide for the registration and regulation of clinical establishments in the country and for matters connected therewith or incidental thereto.

WHEREAS, it is considered expedient to provide for the registration and regulation of clinical establishments with a view to prescribe minimum standards of facilities and services which may be provided by them so that mandate of article 47 of the Constitution for improvement in public health may be achieved;

AND WHEREAS, Parliament has no power to make laws for the States with respect to any of the mattersaforesaid except as provided in articles 249 and 250 of the Constitution;

AND WHEREAS, in pursuance of clause (1) of article 252 of the Constitution, resolutions have been passed by all the Houses of the Legislatures of the States of Arunachal Pradesh, Himachal Pradesh, Mizoram and Sikkim to the effect that the matters aforesaid should be regulated in those States by Parliament by law;

BE it enacted by Parliament in the Sixty-first Year of the Republic of India as follows:—

CHAPTER I - PRELIMINARY

1.   Short title, application and commencement.—(*1*) This Act may be called the Clinical Establishments (Registration and Regulation) Act, 2010.

(2)   It applies, in the first instance, to the whole of the States of Arunachal Pradesh, Himachal Pradesh,Mizoram and Sikkim and the

Union territories; and it shall apply to such other State which adopts thisAct by resolution passed in that behalf under clause (1) of article 252 of the Constitution.

(3)   It shall come into force at once in the States of Arunachal Pradesh, Himachal Pradesh, Mizoram and Sikkim and the Union territories, on such date as the Central Government may, by notification, appoint and in any other State which adopts this Act under clause (1) of article 252 of the Constitution, onthe date of such adoption; and any reference in this Act to the commencement of this Act shall, in relationto any State or Union territory, mean the date on which this Act comes into force in such State or Union territory:

Provided that different dates may be appointed for different categories of clinical establishments and for different recognised systems of medicine.

2.   Definitions.—In this Act, unless the context otherwise requires,—

(a)   "authority" means the district registering authority set-up under section 10;

(b)   "certificate" means certificate of registration issued under section 30;

(c)   "clinical establishment" means—

(i)   a hospital, maternity home, nursing home, dispensary, clinic, sanatorium or an institution by whatever name called that offers services, facilities requiring diagnosis, treatment or care for illness, injury, deformity, abnormality or pregnancy in any recognised system of medicine established and administered or maintained by any person or body of persons, whether incorporated or not; or

(ii)   in sub-clause (i), in connection with the diagnosis or treatment of diseases where pathological, bacteriological, genetic, radiological, chemical, biological investigations or other diagnostic or investigative services with the aid of laboratory or other medical equipment, are usually carried on, established and administered or maintained by any person or body of persons, whether incorporated or not, and shall include a clinical establishment owned, controlled or managed by—

(a)   the Government or a department of the Government;

(b)   a trust, whether public or private;

(c)   a corporation (including a society) registered under a Central, Provincial or State Act, whetheror not owned by the Government;

(d)   a local authority; and

(e)   a single doctor,

but does not include the clinical establishments owned, controlled or managed by the Armed Forces.

Explanation.—For the purpose of this clause "Armed Forces" means the forces constituted under theArmy Act, 1950 (46 of 1950) , the Air Force Act, 1950 (45 of 1950) and the Navy Act, 1957

(62 of 1957);

(d)   "emergency medical condition" means a medical condition manifesting itself by acute symptoms of sufficient severity (including severe pain) of such a nature that the absence of immediatemedical attention could reasonably be expected to result in—

(i)   placing the health of the individual or, with respect to a pregnant women, the health of thewoman or her unborn child, in serious jeopardy; or

(ii)   serious impairment to bodily functions; or

(iii)   serious dysfunction of any organ or part of a body;

(e)   "National Council" means the National Council for clinical establishments established under section 3;

(f)   "notification" means a notification published in the Official Gazette;

(g)   "prescribed" means prescribed by rules made under this Act by the Central Government or, as the case may be, the State Government;

(h)   "recognised system of medicine" means Allopathy, Yoga, Naturopathy, Ayurveda,Homoeopathy, Siddha and Unani System of medicines or any other system of medicine as may be recognised by the Central Government;

(i)   "register" means the register maintained by the authority, State Government and the Central Government under sections 37, 38 and 39 respectively of this Act containing the number of clinical establishments registered;

(j)   "registration" means to register under section 11 and the expression registration or registered shall be construed accordingly;

(k)   "rules" means rules made under this Act;

(l)   "Schedule" means the Schedule appended to this Act;

(m)   "standards" means the conditions that the Central Government may prescribe under section 12, for the registration of clinical establishments;

(n)   "State Government", in relation to a Union territory, means the Administrator thereof appointed under article 239 of the Constitution; and

"to stabilise (with its grammatical variations and cognate expressions)" means, with respect to an emergency medical condition specified in clause (d), to provide such medical treatment of the condition as may be necessary to assure, within reasonable medical probability, that no material deterioration of the condition is likely to result from or occur during the transfer of the individual from a clinical establishment.

CHAPTER II - THE NATIONAL COUNCIL FOR CLINICAL ESTABLISHMENTS

3.   Establishment of National Council.—(1) With effect from such date as the Central Government may, by notification appoint in this behalf, there shall be established for the purposes of this Act, a Council to be called the National Council for clinical establishments.

(2)   The National Council shall consist of—

(a)   Director-General of Health Service, Ministry of Health and Family Welfare, *ex officio,* who shall be the Chairperson;

(b)   four representatives out of which one each to be elected by the—

(i)   Dental Council of India constituted under section 3 of the Dentists Act, 1948 (16 of 1948);

(ii)   Medical Council of India constituted under section 3 of the Indian Medical Council Act,1956 (102 of 1956);

(iii)   Nursing Council of India constituted under section 3 of the Indian Nursing Council Act,1947 (48 of 1947);

(iv)   Pharmacy Council of India constituted under section 3 of the Pharmacy Act, 1948(8 of 1948);

(c)   three representatives to be elected by the Central Council of Indian Medicine representing the Ayurveda, Siddha and Unani systems of medicine constituted under section 3 of the Indian Medicine Central Council Act, 1970 (48 of 1970);

(d)   one representative to be elected by the Central Council of Homoeopathy constituted under section 3 of the Homoeopathy Central Council Act, 1973 (59 of 1973);

(e)   one representative to be elected by the Central Council of the Indian Medical Association;

(f)   one representative of Bureau of the Indian Sandards constituted under section 3 of the Bureauof Indian Standards Act, 1986 (63 of 1986);

(g)   two representatives from the Zonal Council set-up under section 15 of the StatesReorganisation Act, 1956 (37 of 1956);

(h)   two representatives from the North-Eastern Council set-up under section 3 of theNorth-Eastern Council Act, 1971 (84 of 1971);

(i)   one representative from the line of paramedical systems excluding systems that have beengiven representation under clause (*b*);

(j)   two representatives from National Level Consumer Group to be nominated by the CentralGovernment;

(k)   one representative from the Associations of Indian Systems of Medicines relating toAyurveda, Siddha and Unani to be nominated by the Central Government;

(*l*)   the Secretary-General of the Quality Council of India, *ex officio.*

(3)   The nominated members of the National Council shall hold office for three years but shall be eligible for re-nomination for maximum of one more term of three years.

(4)   The elected members of the National Council shall hold office for three years, but shall be eligiblefor re-election:

Provided that the person nominated or elected, as the case may be, shall hold office for such periodtill he holds appointment of the office by virtue of which he was nominated or elected to the council.

(5)   The members of the National Council shall be entitled for such allowances as may be prescribed by the Central Government.

(6)   The National Council may, subject to the previous approval of the Central Government, make bye-laws fixing a quorum and regulating its own procedure and the conduct of all business to be transacted by it.

(7)   The National Council shall meet at least once in three months.

(8)   The National Council may constitute sub-committees and may appoint to such sub-committee, asit deems fit, persons, who are not members of the National Council, for such period, not exceeding two years, for the consideration of particular matters.

(9)   The functions of the National Council may be exercised notwithstanding any vacancy therein.

(10)   The Central Government shall appoint such person to be the Secretary of the National Council as the Central Government may prescribe, and may provide the National Council with such other secretarial and other staff as the Central Government considers necessary.

4.   Disqualifications for appointment as member.—A person shall be disqualified for being appointed as a member of the National Council if he—

(a)   has been convicted and sentenced to imprisonment for an offence which, in the opinion of theCentral Government, involves moral turpitude; or

(b)   is an undischarged insolvent; or

(c)   is of unsound mind and stands so declared by a competent court; or

(d)   has been removed or dismissed from the service of the Government or a Corporation owned or controlled by the Government; or

(e)   has, in the opinion of the Central Government, such financial or other interest in the Council asis likely to affect prejudicially the discharge by him of his functions as a member.

5.   Functions of National Council.—The National Council shall—

(a)   compile and publish a National Register of clinical establishments within two years from thedate of the commencement of this Act;

(b)   classify the clinical establishments into different categories;

(c)   develop the minimum standards and their periodic review;

(d)   determine within a period of two years from its establishment, the first set of standards forensuring proper healthcare by the clinical establishments;

(e)   collect the statistics in respect of clinical establishments;

(f)   perform any other function determined by the Central Government from time to time.

6.   Power to seek advice or assistance.—The National Council may associate with itself any person or body whose assistance or advice it may desire in carrying out any of the provisions of this Act.

7.   National Council to follow consultative process.—The National Council shall follow a consultative process for determining the standards and for classification of clinical establishments in accordance with such procedure as may be prescribed.

CHAPTER III - REGISTRATION AND STANDARDS FOR CLINICAL ESTABLISHMENTS

8.   State Council of clinical establishments.—(*1*) Every State Government shall by notification constitute a State Council for clinical establishments or the Union territory Council for clinical establishments, as the case may be.

(2)   The State Council or the Union territory Council, as the case may be, shall consist of the following members, namely:—

(a)   Secretary, Health—*ex officio*, who shall be the Chairman;

(b)   Director of Health Services—*ex officio* member-secretary;

(c)   Directors of different streams of Indian Systems of Medicine—*ex officio* members;

(d)   one representative each to be elected by the executive committee of—

(i)   State Medical Council of India;

(ii)   State Dental Council of India;

(iii)   State Nursing Council of India;

(iv)   State Pharmacy Council of India;

(e)   three representatives to be elected by the Executive of the State Council or the Union territory Council, as the case may be, of Indian Medicine representing the Ayurveda, Siddha and Unani systems of medicine;

(f)   one representative to be elected by the State Council of the Indian Medical Association;

(g)   one representative from the line of paramedical systems;

(h)   two representatives from State level consumer groups or reputed non-Governmental organisations working in the field of health.

(3)   The nominated member of the State Council or the Union territory Council, as the case may be, shall hold office for a term of three years, but shall be eligible for re-nomination for maximum of one more term of three years.

(4)   The elected members of the State Council or the Union territory Council, as the case may be, shallhold office for three years, but shall be eligible for re-election:

Provided that the person nominated or elected, as the case may be, shall hold office for so long as he holds the appointment of the office by virtue of which he was nominated or elected to the State Council orthe Union territory Council, as the case may be.

(5)   The State Council or the Union territory Council shall perform the following functions, namely:—

(a)   compiling and updating the State Registers of clinical establishment;

(b)   sending monthly returns for updating the National Register;

(c)   representing the State in the National Council;

(d)   hearing of appeals against the orders of the authority; and

(e)   publication on annual basis a report on the state of implementation of standards within their respective States.

9.   Providing information to National Council.—It shall be the responsibility of the State Council for clinical establishments to compile and update the State Register of clinical establishments of the State and further to send monthly returns in digital format for updating the National Register.

10.   Authority for registration.—(*1*) The State Government shall, by notification, set-up an authorityto be called the district registering authority for each district for registration of clinical establishments, with the following members, namely:—

(a)   District Collector— Chairperson;

(b)   District Health Officer—Convenor;

(c)   three members with such qualifications and on such terms and conditions as may be prescribed by the Central Government.

(*2*) Notwithstanding anything contained in sub-section (*1*), for the purposes of provisional registrationof clinical establishments under section 14, the District Health Officer or the Chief Medical Officer (by whatever name called) shall exercise the powers of the authority as per procedure that may be prescribed.

11.   Registration for clinical establishments.—No person shall run a clinical establishment unless it has been duly registered in accordance with the provisions of this Act.

12.   Condition for registration.—(*1*) For registration and continuation, every clinical establishment shall fulfil the following conditions, namely:—

(i)   the minimum standards of facilities and services as may be prescribed;

(ii)   the minimum requirement of personnel as may be prescribed;

(iii)   provisions for maintenance of records and reporting as may be prescribed;

(iv)   such   other   conditions   as   may   be   prescribed.

(*2*) The clinical establishment shall undertake to provide within the staff and facilities available, such medical examination and treatment as may be required to stabilise the emergency medical condition of any individual who comes or is brought to such clinical establishment.

13.   Classification of clinical establishments.—(*1*) Clinical establishment of different systems shall be classified into such categories, as may be prescribed by the Central Government, from time to time.

(*2*) Different standards may be prescribed for classification of different categories referred to in sub-section (*1*):

Provided that in prescribing the standards for clinical establishments, the Central Government shall have regard to the local conditions.

CHAPTERIV - PROCEDURE FOR REGISTRATION

14.   Application for provisional certificate of registration.—(*1*) For the purposes of registration of the clinical establishment under section 10, an application in the prescribed proforma along with the prescribed fee shall be made to the authority.

(2)   The application shall be filed in person or by post or online.

(3)   The application shall be made in such form and shall be accompanied by such details as may be prescribed under this Act or rules made thereunder.

(4)   If any clinical establishment is in existence at the time of the

commencement of this Act, an application for its registration shall be made within one year from the date of the commencement of this Act and a clinical establishment which comes into existence after commencement of this Act, shall apply for permanent registration within a period of six months from the date of its establishment.

(5) If any clinical establishment is already registered under any existing law requiring registration of such establishments, even then it shall apply for registration as referred to in sub-section (*1*).

15. Provisional certificate.—The authority shall, within a period of ten days from the date of receipt of such application, grant to the applicant a certificate of provisional registration in such form and containing such particulars and such information, as may be prescribed.

16. No inquiry prior to provisional registration.—(*1*) The authority shall not conduct any inquiry prior to the grant of provisional registration.

(*2*) Notwithstanding the grant of the provisional certificate of registration, the authority shall, within aperiod of forty-five days from the grant of provisional registration, cause to be published in such manner, as may be prescribed, all particulars of the clinical establishment so registered provisionally.

17. Validity of provisional registration.—Subject to the provisions of section 23, every provisional registration shall be valid to the last day of the twelfth month from the date of issue of the certificate of registration and such registration shall be renewable.

18. Display of certificate of registration.—The certificate shall be kept affixed in a conspicuous place in the clinical establishment in such manner so as to be visible to every one visiting such establishment.

19. Duplicate certificate.—In case the certificate is lost, destroyed, mutilated or damaged, theauthority shall issue a duplicate certificate on the request of the clinical establishment and on the paymentof such fees as may be prescribed.

20. Certificate to be non-transferable.—(*1*) The certificate of registration shall be non-transferable.

(2)   In the event of change of ownership or management, the clinical establishment shall inform the authority of such change in such manner as may be prescribed.

(3)   In the event of change of category, or location, or on ceasing to function as a clinical establishment, the certificate of registration in respect of such clinical establishment shall be surrendered to the authority and the clinical establishment shall apply afresh for grant of certificate of registration.

21.   Publication of expiry of registration.—The authority shall cause to be published within such time and in such manner, as may be prescribed, the names of clinical establishments whose registration has expired.

22.   Renewal of registration.—The application for renewal of registration shall be made thirty days before the expiry of the validity of the certificate of provisional registration and, in case the application for renewal is made after the expiry of the provisional registration, the authority shall allow renewal of registration on payment of such enhanced fees, as may be prescribed.

23.   Time limit for provisional registration.—Where the clinical establishments in respect of which standards have been notified by the Central Government, provisional registration shall not be granted or renewed beyond,—

(i)   the period of two years from the date of notification of the standards in case of clinical establishments which came into existence before the commencement of this Act;

(ii)   the period of two years from the date of notification of the standards for clinical establishments which come into existence after the commencement of this Act but before the notification of the standards; and the period of six months from the date of notification of standards for clinical establishments which come into existence after standards have been notified.

24.   Application for permanent registration.—Application for permanent registration by a clinical establishment shall be made to the authority in such form and be accompanied by such fees, as may be prescribed.

25.   Verification of application.—The clinical establishment shall submit evidence of having complied with the prescribed minimum standards in such manner, as may be prescribed.

26.   Display of information for filing objections.—As soon as the clincial establishment submits the required evidence of having complied with the prescribed minimum standards, the authority shall cause tobe displayed for information of the public at large and for filing objections, if any, in such manner, as maybe prescribed, all evidence submitted by the clinical establishment of having complied with the prescribed minimum standards for a period of thirty days before processing for grant of permanent registration.

27.   Communication of objections.—If objections are received within the period referred to in the preceding section, such objections shall be communicated to the clinical establishment for response within a period of forty-five days.

28.   Standards   for   permanent   registration.—Permanent registration shall be granted only when a clinical establishment fulfils the prescribed standards for registration by the Central Government.

29.   Allowing or disallowing of registration.—The authority shall pass an order immediately after the expiry of the prescribed period and within the next thirty days thereafter either—

(a)   allowing the application for permanent registration; or

(b)   disallowing the application:

Provided that the authority shall record its reasons, if it disallows an application, for permanent registration.

30.   Certificate of permanent registration.—(*1*) The authority shall, if it, allows an application ofthe clinical establishment, issue a certificate of permanent registration in such form and containing such particulars, as may be prescribed.

(2)   The certificate shall be valid for a period of five years from the date of issue.

(3)   For the purposes of sub-section (*1*), the provisions of sections 18, 19, 20 and 21 shall also apply.

(4)   The applications for renewal of permanent registration shall be made within six months before the expiry of the validity of the certificate of permanent registration and, in case the application of renewal is not submitted within the stipulated period, the authority may allow renewal of registration on payment of such enhanced fees and penalties as may be prescribed.

31.   Fresh application for permanent registration.—The disallowing of an application for permanent registration shall not debar a clinical establishment from applying afresh for permanentregistration under section 24 and after providing such evidence, as may be required, of having rectifiedthe deficiences on which grounds the earlier application was disallowed.

32.   Cancellation of registration.—(*1*) If, at any time after any clinical establishment has been registered, the authority is satisfied that,—

(a)   the conditions of the registration are not being complied with; or

(b)   the person entrusted with the management of the clinical establishment has been convicted of an offence punishable under this Act,

it may issue a notice to the clinical establishment to show cause within three months' time as to why its registration under this Act should not be cancelled for the reasons to be mentioned in the notice.

(2)   If after giving a reasonable opportunity to the clinical establishment, the authority is satisfied that there has been a breach of any of the provisions of this Act or the rules made thereunder, it may, by an order, without prejudice to any other action that it may take against such clinical establishment, cancel its registration.

(3)   Every order made under sub-section (*2*) shall take effect—

(a)   where no appeal has been preferred against such order immediately on the expiry of the periodprescribed for such appeal; and

(b)   where such appeal has been preferred and it has been dismissed from the date of the order of such dismissal:

Provided that the authority, after cancellation of registration for reasons to be recorded in writing,may restrain immediately the clinical establishment from carrying on if there is imminent danger to the health and safety of patients.

33. **Inspection of registered clinical establishments.**—(*1*) The authority or an officer authorised by it shall have the right to cause an inspection of, or inquiry in respect of any registered clinical establishment, its building, laboratories and equipment and also of the work conducted or done by the clinical establishment, to be made by such multi-member inspection team as it may direct and to cause an inquiry to be made in respect of any other matter connected with the clinical establishment and that establishment shall be entitled to be represented thereat.

(2) The authority shall communicate to the clinical establishment the views of that authority with reference to the results of such inspection or inquiry and may, after ascertaining the opinion of the clinical establishment thereon, advise that establishment upon the action to be taken.

(3) The clinical establishment shall report to the authority, the action, if any, which is proposed to be taken or has been taken upon the results of such inspection or inquiry and such report shall be furnished within such time, as the authority may direct.

(4) Where the clinical establishment does not, within a reasonable time, take action to the satisfaction of the authority, it may, after considering any explanation furnished or representation made by the clinical establishment, issue such directions within such time as indicated in the direction, as that authority deems fit, and the clinical establishment shall comply with such directions.

34. **Power to enter.**—The authority or an officer authorised by it may, if there is any reason to suspect that anyone is carrying on a clinical establishment without registration, enter and search in the manner prescribed, at any reasonable time and the clinical establishment, shall offer reasonable facilities for inspection or inquiry and be entitled to be represented thereat:

Provided that no such person shall enter the clinical establishment without giving notice of his intention to do so.

35.   Levy   of   fee   by   State   Government.—The   State Government   may   charge   fees   for   different categories   of   clinical establishments, as may be prescribed.

36.   Appeal.—(*1*) Any person, aggrieved by an order of the registering authority refusing to grant or renew a certificate of registration or revoking a certificate of registration may, in such manner and within such period as may be prescribed, prefer an appeal to the State Council:

Provided that the State Council may entertain an appeal preferred after the expiry of the prescribed period if it is satisfied that the appellant was prevented by sufficient cause from preferring the appeal in time.

(*2*) Every appeal under sub-section (*1*) shall be made in such form and be accompanied by such fee as may be prescribed

CHAPTER   V   -   REGISTER   OF   CLINICAL ESTABLISHMENTS

37.   Register of clinical establishments.—(*1*) The authority shall within a period of two years from its establishment, compile, publish and maintain in digital format a register of clinical establishments, registered by it and it shall enter the particulars of the certificate so issued in a register to be maintained in such form and manner, as may be prescribed by the State Government.

(*2*) Each authority, including any other authority set-up for the registration of clinical establishments under any other law for the time being in force, shall supply in digital format to the State Council of clinical establishments a copy of every entry made in the register of clinical establishments in such manner, as may be prescribed to ensure that the State Register is constantly up-to-date with the registers maintained by the registering authority in the State.

38.   Maintenance   of   State   Register   of   clinical establishments.—(*1*) Every State Government shall maintain in digital and in such form and containing such particulars, as may be prescribed by the Central Government a register to be known as the

State Register of clinical establishments in respect of clinical establishments of that State.

(2) Every State Government shall supply in digital format to the Central Government, a copy of the State Register of clinical establishments and shall inform the Central Government all additions to and other amendments in such register made, for a particular month by the 15th day of the following month.

39. Maintenance of National Register of clinical establishments.—The Central Government shall maintain in digital format an All India Register to be called as the National Register of clinical establishments that shall be an amalgam of the State Register of clinical establishments maintained by the State Governments and shall cause the same to be published in digital format.

CHAPTERVI - PENALTIES

40. Penalty.—Whoever contravenes any provision of this Act shall, if no penalty is provided elsewhere, be punishable for the first offence with fine which may extend to ten thousand rupees, for any second offence with fine which may extend to fifty thousand rupees and for any subsequent offence with fine which may extend to five lakh rupees.

41. Monetary penalty for non-registration.—(1) Whoever carries on a clinical establishment without registration shall, on first contravention, be liable to a monetary penalty up to fifty thousand rupees, for second contravention with a monetary penalty which may extend to two lakh rupees and for any subsequent contravention with a monetary penalty which may extend to five lakh rupees.

(2) Whoever knowingly serves in a clinical establishment which is not duly registered under this Act, shall be liable to a monetary penalty which may extend to twenty-five thousand rupees.

(3) For the purpose of adjudging under sub-sections (1) and (2), the authority shall hold an inquiry in the prescribed manner after giving any person concerned a reasonable opportunity of being heard for the purpose of imposing any monetary penalty.

(4)   While holding an inquiry the authority shall have power to summon and enforce the attendance of any person acquainted with the facts and circumstances of the case to give evidence or to produce any document which in the opinion of the authority, may be useful for or relevant to the subject matter of the inquiry and if, on such inquiry, it is satisfied that the person has failed to comply with the provisions specified in sub-sections (1) and (2), it may by order impose the monetary penalty specified in those sub-sections to be deposited within thirty days of the order in the account referred to in sub-section (8) of section 42.

(5)   While determining the quantum of monetary penalty, the authority shall take into account the category, size and type of the clinical establishment and local conditions of the area in which the establishment is situated.

(6)   Any person aggrieved by the decision of the authority may prefer an appeal to the State Council within a period of three months from the date of the said decision.

(7)   The manner of filing the appeal referred to in sub-section (6) shall be such as may be prescribed.

42.   Disobedience of direction, obstruction and refusal of information.—(1) Whoever wilfully disobeys any direction lawfully given by any person or authority empowered under this Act to give such direction, or obstructs any person or authority in the discharge of any functions which such person or authority is required or empowered under this Act to discharge, shall be liable to a monetary penalty which may extend to five lakh rupees.

(2)   Whoever being required by or under this Act to supply any information wilfully withholds such information or gives information which he knows to be false or which he does not believe to be true, shallbe liable to a monetary penalty which may extend to five lakh rupees.

(3)   For the purpose of adjudging under sub-sections (1) and (2), the authority shall hold an inquiry in the prescribed manner after giving any person concerned a reasonable opportunity of being heard for the purpose of imposing any monetary penalty.

(4)   While holding an inquiry the authority shall have power to summon and enforce the attendance of any person acquainted with the facts and circumstances of the case to give evidence or to produce any document which in the opinion of the authority, may be useful for or relevant to the subject matter of the inquiry and if, on such inquiry, it is satisfied that the person has failed to comply with the provisions specified in sub-sections (1) and (2), it may by order impose the monetary penalty specified in those sub-sections to be deposited within thirty days of the order in the account referred to in sub-section (8).

(5)   While determining the quantum of monetary penalty, the authority shall take into account the category, size and type of the clinical establishment and local conditions of the area in which the establishment is situated.

(6)   Any person aggrieved by the decision of the authority may prefer an appeal to the State Council within a period of three months from the date of the said decision.

(7)   The manner of filing the appeal referred to in sub-section (6) shall be such as may be prescribed.

(8)   The monetary penalty levied under sections 41 and 42 shall be credited to such account as the State Government may by order specify in this behalf.

43.   Penalty for minor deficiencies.—Whoever contravenes any provision of this Act or any rule made thereunder resulting in deficiencies that do not pose any imminent danger to the health and safety of any patient and can be rectified within a reasonable time, shall be punishable with fine which may extend to ten thousand rupees.

44.   Contravention by companies.—(1) Where a person committing contravention of any of the provisions of this Act or of any rule made thereunder is a company, every person who, at the time the contravention was committed, was in charge of, and was responsible to the company for the conduct of the business of the company, as well as the company, shall be deemed to be guilty of the contravention and shall be liable to fine: Provided that nothing contained in this sub-section shall render any such person liable to any punishment if he proves that the contravention was committed without his knowledge or that he had exercised all due diligence to prevent the commission of such contravention.

(2)   Notwithstanding anything contained in sub-section (*1*), where a contravention of any of the provisions of this Act or of any rule made thereunder has been committed by a company and it is proved that the contravention has taken place with the consent or connivance of, or is attributable to any neglect on the part of, any director, manager, secretary or other officer of the company, such director, manager, secretary or other officer shall also be deemed to be guilty of that contravention and shall be liable to fine.

Explanation.—For the purpose of this section,—

(a)   "company" means a body corporate and includes a firm or other association of individuals; and

(b)   "director", in relation to a firm, means a partner in the firm.

45.   Offences by Government Departments.—(*1*) Where an offence under this Act has been committed by any Department of Government within a period of six months after the commencement of this Act, the Head of the Department shall be deemed to be guilty of the offence and shall be liable to be proceeded against and punished accordingly:

Provided that nothing contained in this section shall render such Head of the Department liable to anypunishment if he proves that the offence was committed without his knowledge or that he exercised alldue diligence to prevent the commission of such offence.

(*2*) Notwithstanding anything contained in sub-section (*1*), where an offence under this Act has been committed by a Department of Government and it is proved that the offence has been committed with the consent or connivance of, or is attributable to any neglect on the part of, any officer, other than the Head of the Department, such officer shall also be deemed to be guilty of that offence and shall be liable to be proceeded against and punished accordingly.

46.   Recovery of fine.—Whoever fails to pay the fine, the State Council of clinical establishment mayprepare a certificate signed by an officer authorised by it specifying the fine due from such person and send it to the Collector of the District in which such person owns any property or resides or carries on his business and the said Collector, on receipt of such certificate, shall proceed to recover from such person the amount specified thereunder, as if it were an arrear of land revenue.

CHAPTER VII MISCELLANEOUS

47. **Protection of action taken in good faith.**—(*1*) No suit, prosecution or other legal proceedings shall lie against any authority or any member of the National Council or State Council or any officer authorised in this behalf in respect of anything, which is in good faith done or intended to be done in pursuance of the provisions of this Act or any rule made thereunder.

48. (*2*) No suit or other legal proceedings shall lie against a State Government or the Central Government in respect of any loss or damage caused or likely to be caused by anything which is in good faith done or intended to be done in pursuance of the provisions of this Act or any rule made thereunder.

49. **Furnishing of returns, etc.**—Every clinical establishment shall, within such time or within such extended time, as may be prescribed in that behalf, furnish to the authority or the State Council or the National Council such returns or the statistics and other information in such manner, as may be prescribed by the State Government, from time to time.

50. **Power to give directions.**—Without prejudice to the foregoing provisions of this Act, the authority shall have the power to issue such directions, including furnishing returns, statistics and other information for the proper functioning of clinical establishments and such directions shall be binding.

51. **Employees of the authority, etc., to be public servants.**—Every employee of the authority, the National Council and the State Council shall be deemed to, when acting or purporting to act in pursuance of any of the provisions of this Act, be public servants within the meaning of section 21 of the Indian Penal Code (45 of

1860).

52.   Power to remove difficulties.—(*1*) If any difficulty arises in giving effect to the provisions of this Act, the Central Government may, by order published in the Official Gazette, make such provisions not inconsistent with the provisions of this Act as may appear to it to be necessary or expedient for removal of the difficulty:

Provided that no such order shall be made after the expiry of a period of two years from the date of commencement of this Act.

(*2*) Every order made under this section shall, as soon as may be after it is made, be laid before each House of Parliament.

53.   Power of Central Government to make rules.—(*1*) The Central Government may, by notification, make rules for carrying out all or any of the provisions of this Act.

(2)   In particular and without prejudice to the generality of the foregoing power, such rules may provide for all or any of the following matters, namely:—

(a)   allowances for the members of the National Council under sub-section (*5*) of section 3;

(b)   appointment of such person to be the Secretary of the State Council by the Central Government under sub-section (*10*) of section 3;

(c)   the determination of standards and for classification of clinical establishments under section 7;

(d)   the qualification and the terms and conditions for the members of the authority under clause © of sub-section (*1*) of section 10;

(d)   the procedure under which the powers of the authority may be exercised by the District Health Officer or Chief Medical Officer for the purpose of provisional registration of clinical establishment under sub-section (*2*) of section 10;

(e)   the minimum standards of facilities and services under clause (*i*) of sub-section (*1*) of section 12

(f)   the minimum number of personnel under clause (*ii*) of sub-section (*1*) of section 12;

(g)   the maintenance of records and reporting by the clinical establishment under clause *(iii)* of

(h)   other conditions for registration and continuation of clinical establishment under clause *(iv)* ofsub-section (*1*) of section 12;

(i)   classification of clinical establishment under sub-section (*1*) of section 13;

(j)   the different standards for classification of clinical establishments under sub-section (*2*) ofsection 13;

(k)   the minimum standards for permanent registration under section 28;

(l)   the form and particulars to be contained in the register to be maintained under section 38.

54.   **Laying of rules.**—Every rule made by the Central Government under this Act shall be laid, as soon as may be after it is made, before each House of Parliament, while it is in session, for a total period of thirty days which may be comprised in one session or in two or more successive sessions and if, before the expiry of the session immediately following the session or the successive sessions aforesaid, both Houses agree in making any modification in the rule or both Houses agree that the rule should not be made, the rule shall thereafter have effect only in such modified form or be of no effect, as the case may be; so, however, that any such modification or annulment shall be without prejudice to the validity of anything previously done under that rule.

55.   **Power of State Government to make rules.**—(*1*) The State Government may, by notification, make rules for carrying out in respect of matters which do not fall within the purview of section 52.

(2)   In particular and without prejudice to the generality of the foregoing power, such rules may provide for all or any of the following matters, namely:—

(a)   the proforma and the fee to be paid for registration under sub-section (*1*) of section 14;

(b)   the form and details of application under sub-section (*3*) of

section 14;

(c)   the particulars and information contained in certificate of provisional registration undersection 15;

(d)   the manner of publication of all particulars of the clinical establishments proposed to beregistered under sub-section *(2)* of section 16;

(e)   the fees to be paid to issue a duplicate certificate under section 19;

(f)   the change of ownership or management to be informed by the clinical establishment to theauthority under sub-section *(2)* of section 20;

(g)   the manner in which the authority shall publish the names of the clinical establishments whoseregistration expired under section 21;

(h)   the enhanced fees to be charged for renewal after expiry of the provisional registration undersection 22;

(i)   the form of the application and fees to be charged by the State Government under section 24;

(j)   the manner of submitting evidence of the clinical establishments having complied with theminimum standards under section 25;

(k)   the manner of displaying information of the clinical establishments having complied with theminimum standards for filing objection under section 26;

(l)   the expiry of period specified in section 29;

(m)   the form and particulars of the certificate of registration under section 30;

(n)   the period within which an appeal shall be preferred under clause *(a)* of sub-section *(3)* ofsection 32;

(o)   the manner of entry and search of clinical establishment under section 34;

(p)   the fees to be charged by the State Government for different categories of clinicalestablishments under section 35;

(q)   the manner and the period within which an appeal may be preferred to the State Council undersub-section *(1)* of section 36;

(r)   the form and the fee to be paid for an appeal under sub-section *(2)* of section 36;

(s)   the form and the manner in which the register to be maintained under sub-section *(1)* ofsection 37;

the manner of supply to the State Council in digital format the entry made in the register ofclinical establishment under sub-section *(2)* of section 37;

(t)   the manner of holding an inquiry by the authority under sub-section *(3)* of sections 41 and 42;

(u)   the manner of filing the appeal under sub-section *(7)* of sections 41 and 42;

(v)   the manner and the time within which the information is to be furnished to the authority or theState Council or the National Council as the case may be, under section 48;

(w)   any other matter which is required to be or may be prescribed by the State Government.

56.   Laying of rules.—Every rule made by the State Government under this section shall be laid, as soon as may be after it is made, before each House of the State Legislature where it consists of two Houses, or where such Legislature consists of one House, before that House.

57.   Savings.—*(1)* The provisions of this Act shall not apply to the States in which the enactments specified in the Schedule are applicable:

Provided that the States in which the enactments referred to in sub-section *(1)* are applicable, and such States subsequent to the commencement of this Act, adopts this Act under clause (1) of article 252of the Constitution, the provisions of this Act shall, subsequent to such adoption, apply in that State.

(2) The Central Government may, as and when consider necessary, by notification amend the Schedule.

THE SCHEDULE

[*See* section 56]

1.   The Andhra Pradesh Private Medical Care Establishments (Registration and Regulation) Act, 2002.

2.   The Bombay Nursing Homes Registration Act, 1949.

3.   The Delhi Nursing Homes Registration Act, 1953.

4.   The Madhya Pradesh Upcharya Griha Tatha Rujopchar Sanbabdu Sthapamaue (RagistrikaranTatha Anugyapan) Adhiniyam, 1973.

5.   The Manipur Homes and Clinics Registration Act, 1992.

6.   The Nagaland Health Care Establishments Act, 1997.

7.   The Orissa Clinical Establishments (Control and Regulation) Act, 1990.

8.   The Punjab State Nursing Home Registration Act, 1991.

Maharashtra The Bombay Nursing Homes Registration Act, 1949

CONTENTS

PREAMBLESECTIONS

The Bombay Nursing Homes Registration Act 1949

[6th May 1949]

An Act to provide for the registration and inspection of nursing Homes in the Province of Bombay and for certain purpose Connected therewith.

WHEREAS it is expedient to provide for the registration and inspection of nursinghomes in the Province of Bombay and for certain purposes connected therewith; It is hereby enacted as follows: -

1.   (1) This Act may be called the Bombay Nursing Homes RegistrationAct,1949.

(2) This section extends to the whole of the Province of Bombay. The remaining provisions of this Act extend in the first instance to the Greater Bombay and the areas within the limits of the Municipal Boroughs of Ahmedabad, Poona City, Poona Suburban and Sholapea and the Provincial Government may, by notification in the Official Gazette, direct that the said provisions shall extend to such other areas as may be specified in the notification.

(3) This section shall come into force at once. The Provincial Governmentmay, by notification in the Official Gazette, direct that the remainingprovisions of this Act shall come into force in any area to which the said provisions extend or may have been extended under sub-section (2) on such date as may be specified in the notification

2. In this Act, unless there is anything repugnant in the subject or context

(1) "By-laws" means by-laws made by the local supervising authority;

(2) "Local supervising authority" in the case of a municipal area

means the municipality established for such area , and in the case ofany other area a district local board established for the said area;

(3) "Maternity home" means any premises used, or intended to be used, for the reception of pregnant women or of women in or immediately after child birth;

(4) "Nursing home" means any premises used or intended to be used, for the reception of persons suffering from any sickness, injury or infirmity and the providing to treatment and nursing for them, and includes a maternity home; and the expression "to carry on a nursing home" means to receive persons in a nursing home for any of the aforesaid purposes and to providetreatment or nursing for them;

(5) "Prescribed" means prescribed by rules made under this Act;

(6) "Qualified medical practitioner" means a medical practitioner registeredunder the Bombay Medical Act, 1912, or any other law for the time being in force;

(7) "Qualified midwife" means a midwife registered under the BombayNurses, Midwives and Health Visitors Registration Act, 1935

(8) "Qualified nurse" means a nurse registered under the Bombay Nurses,Midwives and Health Visitors Registration Act, 1935.

(9) "register" means to register under section 5 of this Act and the expressions "registered" and "registration" shall be construed accordingly;

(10) "Rules" means rules made under this Act.

3. No person shall carry on a nursing home unless he has been duly registered in respect of such nursing home and the registration in respect thereof has not been cancelled under section 7:

Provided that nothing in the section shall apply in the case of a nursing home which, is in existence at the date of the commencement of this Act, for a period of three months from such date or if an application for registration is made within that period in accordance with the provisions of section 4 until such application is finally disposed of.

4. (1) Every person intending to carry on a nursing home shall

make every year an application for registration or the renewal of registration to the local supervising authority:

Provided that in the case of a nursing home which is in existence at the date of the commencement of this Act an application for registration shall be made within three months from such date.

(2) Every application for registration or the renewal of registration shall be made on such date and in such form and shall be accompanied, by such fee, as may be prescribed.

5.   (1) Subject to the provisions of this Act and the rules , the local supervising authority shall, on the receipt of an application for registration, register the applicant in respect of the nursing home named in the application and issue to him a certificate of registration in the prescribed form:

Provided that the local supervising authority may refuse to register the applicant if it is satisfied:

(a)   That he, or any person employed by him at the nursing home, is not a fit person, whether by reason of age or otherwise, to carry on or to be employed at a nursing home of such a description as the nursing home named in the application; or

(b)   That the nursing home is not under the management of a person who is either a qualified medical practitioner or a qualified nurse and who is resident in the home, or that there is not approver proportion of qualified nurses among the persons having the superintendence of or employed in the nursing of the patients in the home; or

(c)   That in the case of a maternity home it has not got on its staff a qualified midwife; or

(d)   That for reasons connected with the situation, constriction, accommodation, staffing or equipment, the nursing home or any premises used in connection therewith are not fit to be used for a nursing home of such a description as the nursing home mentioned in the application or that the nursing home or premises are used or are to be used for purposes which are in any way improper or undesirable in the case of such nursing home.

(2)   A certificate of registration issue under this section shall, subject to the provisions of section 7, be in force and shall be valid until the 31st day of March next following the date on which such certificate was issued.

(3)   The certificate of registration issued in respect of nursing home shall bekept affixed in a conspicuous place in the nursing home.

6.   Whoever contravenes the provisions of section 3, shall, on conviction, bepunished with fine which may extend to five hundred rupees or, in the case of a second or subsequent offence, with imprisonment for a term which may extend to three months or with fine which may extend to five hundred rupees or with both.

7.   Subject to the provisions of this Act, the local supervising authority may atany time cancel the registration of a person in respect of any nursing home on any ground which would entitle ti to refuse an application for the registration of that person in respect of that home, or on the ground that that person has been convicted of an offence under this Act or that any other person has been convicted of such an offence in respect of that home.

8.   (1) Before making an order refusing an application for registration or an ordercanceling any registration, the local supervising authority shall give to the applicant or to the person registered, as the case may be, not less than one calendar month's notice of its intention to make such an order, and every such notice shall state the ground on which the local supervising authority intends to make the order and shall contain an intimation that if within a calendar month after the receipt of the notice the applicant or pers on registered informs the authority in writing that he desires so to do, thelocal supervising authority shall, before making the order, give him (in person or by representative) an opportunity of showing cause why the order should not be made.

(2)   If the local supervising authority, after giving the applicant or the personregistered an opportunity of showing cause as aforesaid, decides to refuse the application for registration or to cancel the registration, as the case may be, it shall make an order to that effect and shall send a copy of the order by registered post to the applicant or the person registered.

(3)   Any person aggrieved by an order refusing an application for registrationor canceling any registration may, within a calendar month after the date on which the copy of the order was sent to him, appeal to the Provincial Government against such order of refusal. The decision of the Provincial Government on any such appeal shall be final.

(4)   No such order shall come into force until after the expiration of a calendar month from the date on which it was made or, where notice of appeal is given against it, until the appeal has been decided or withdrawn.

9.   (1) The Health Officer of the local supervising authority or the Civil Surgeonof the district in which a nursing home is situated or any other officer duly authorised by the local supervising authority or the Civil Surgeon, may, subject to such general or special orders as may be made by the local supervising authority, at all reasonable times enter and inspect and premises which are used, or which that officer has reasonable cause to believe to be used, for the purpose of nursing home, and inspect any records required to be kept in accordance with the provisions of this Act:

Provided that nothing in this Act shall be deemed to authorise any such officer to inspect any medical record relating to any patient in a nursing home.

(2)   If any person refused to allow any such officer to enter or inspect any such premises as aforesaid, or to inspect any such records as aforesaid or abstracts any such officer in the execution of his powers under this section,he shall be guilty of an office under this Act.

10.   Any fees received under this Act shall be paid into the fund of the localsupervising authority.

11.   Notwithstanding anything contained in any enactment in regard to any municipal or local fund, all expenses incurred by a local supervising authority under and for the purposes of this Act and the rules and by-laws may be paid out of the municipal or local fund, as the case may be.

12.   Whoever contravenes any of the provisions of this Act or of any rule shall, if no other penalty is elsewhere provided in this Act or

the rules for suchcontravention, on conviction, be punished with fine which may extend to fifty rupees and in the case of a continuing offence to a further fine of fifteenrupees in respect of each day on which the offence continues after suchconviction.

13.   Where a person committing an offence under this Act is a company or other body corporate or an association of persons (whether incorporated or not), every person who at the time of the commission of the offence was a director, manager, secretary, agent or other officer or person concerned with the management thereof shall, unless he proves that the offence was committed without his knowledge or consent, be deemed to be guilty of such offence.

14.   No court other than that of a Presidency Magistrate or a Magistrate of the firstclass shall take cognizance of or try any offence under this Act.

15.   No suit, prosecution or other legal proceeding shall be instituted against anyperson for anything which is in good faith done or intended to be done under this Act, rules or by-laws.

16.   (1) The Provincial Government may, by notification in the Official Gazette,make person for anything which is in good faith done or intended to be done under this Act, rules or by-laws.

(2)   Without prejudice to the generality of the foregoing provisions such rulesmay prescribe -

(a)   The form of the application to be made under section 4.

(b)   The date on which an application for registration or renewal ofregistration to be made and the fees to be paid for such registration orrenewal of registration,

(c)   The form of the certificate of registration to be issued under section 5.

(d)   For any other matter for which no provision has been made in thisAct, and for which provision is, in the opinion of the Provincial Government, necessary.

(3)   The power to make rules   under   this section shall be subject tothe condition of previous publication in the

Official Gazette.

17.   (1) The local supervising authority may make by-laws not inconsistent withthis Act or rules -

(a)   Prescribing the records to be kept of the patients received into anursing home, and in the case of the maternity home, of miscarriages, abortions or still births occurring in the nursing home and of the children born therein and of the children so born who are removed from the home otherwise than to the custody or care of any parent, guardian relative.

(b)   Requiring notification to be given of any death occurring in the nursinghome.

(2)   Any by-law made by a local supervising authority under this Act mayprovide that a contravention thereof shall be punishable:

(a)   With fine which may extend to fifty rupees; or

(b)   With fine which may extend to fifty rupees and in the case of acontinuing contravention, with an additional fine which may extend to fifteen rupees for every day during which such contravention continues after conviction, for the first such contravention; or

(c)   With fine which may extend to fifteen rupees for every day duringwhich the contravention continues after the receipt of a notice from thelocal supervising authority by the person contravening the by-law requiring such person to discontinue such contravention.

(d)   No by-law made by the local supervising authority shall come intoforce until it has been confirmed by the Provincial Government with orwithout modification.

(4) All by-means under this section shall be published in the official Gazette.

18.   Nothing in this Act shall apply to -

(i)   any nursing home carried on by Government or a local authority or byany other body of persons approved by the Provincial Government in this behalf; and

(ii)   Any asylum for lunatics or patients suffering from mental diseases,within the meaning of the Indian Lunacy Act, 1912.

IN DEVELOPMENT, PUBLIC AND HOUSING DEPARTMENT

Sachivalaya, Bombay-32, 10th May 1973
BOMBAY NURSING HOMES REGISTRATION RULES, 1973

No. NHM. 1161/33950/39497-GII – In exercise of the powers conferred by sub- section (1) and clauses (a) to (d) of sub-section (2) of section of the Bombay Nursing Homes Registration Act, 1949 (Bomb. XV of 1949), and of all other powers enabling itin that behalf, the Government of Maharashtra hereby make the following rules, the same having been previously published as required by subsection (1) of the said section 16, namely: -

I-GENERAL
Short title – These rules may be called the Maharashtra Nursing HomesRegistration Rules, 1973

1.   Definitions – In these rules, unless the context requires otherwise -

(a)   "Act" means the Bombay Nursing Homes Registration Act, 1949;

(b)   "Form" means a forth appended to the rules; and

(c)   "Section" means a section of the Act.

II-MAINTENANCE OF REGISTER

2.   Register – The local supervising authority shall maintain a register in Form 'A'showing the names of persons registered under section 5

3.   Application for registration – Any person intending to carry on a nursing homeshall make an application to the local supervising authority in Form 'B' atleast one month before the date on which he intends to carry on such a nursinghome. Such application shall be

accompanied by a fee prescribed in sub-rule

(1) of rule 7.

4.   Grant of certificate of registration – the local supervising authority shall if satisfied that there is no objection to registration, register the applicant in respect of a nursing home and issue to him a certificate of registration in Form 'C'

5.   Renewal of registration – An application for the renewal of registration shall be made every year in advance in Form 'B' in the month of January, and shall be accompanied by the fee prescribed in sub-rule of rule 7.

6.   Fees for registration and renewal of registration –

(1)   The fees to be paid for registration shall be charged as under:
-

(a)   Rs. 20 in respect of a nursing home having not more than 10 beds;

(b)   Rs. 50 in respect of a nursing home having more that 10 beds.

(2)   The fees for the renewal of registration, shall in each case, be one-half ofthe amount payable for the first registration.

7.   Transfer of ownership etc. of nursing home – Immediately the transfer of the ownership or management of nursing home the transferor and the transferee shall jointly communicate the transfer effected to the local supervising authority and the transferee shall make an application for registration in accordance with the provisions of rule 4

16.   Change of address – A person registered under the Act in respect of a nursinghome shall communicate to the local supervising authority any change in his address or in the situation of the nursing home in respect of which he is registered not later that seventy-two hours after such change.

17.   Change in staff – Any change in the medical, nursing or midwifery staff together with the dates on which such changes has taken place shall becommunicated to the local supervising authority

immediately and in any case, not later than three days of such change.

11. Lost certificate – In the event of certificate of registration being

or destroyed, the holder may apply to the local supervising authority for a fresh certificate and the local supervising authority may, if it thinks fit, issue such certificate upon payment of a fee of Rs. 5 A certificate issued under this rule shall be marked "Duplicate."

MUNICIPAL CORPORATION OF GREATER BOMBAY PUBLIC HEALTH DEPARTMENT NOTIFICATION MDA. 4029

The following by-laws framed in exercise of powers conferred by sub-sections (1) and (2) of section 17 of the Maharashtra (Bombay) Nursing Home Registration Act, 1949and approved by the Municipal Corporation of Greater Bombay by their Resolution No. 374 of 4th August, 1955 and confirmed by the Government of Maharashtra (Bombay)vide letter No. NMH. 1057/49231-D dated 3rd February, 1968, from the Deputy Secretaryto the Government of Bombay Local self-government and Public Health Department as required by Sub-section (3) of Section 17 of the said Act are published herewith as required by sub-section (4) of section 17 of the said act.

These bylaws shall come into force from the date of publication in the Government Gazette:

By-Laws

I.   Short title and extent: -

(1)   These bylaws may be called the Bombay Municipal CorporationNursing Homes Registration by-laws, 1954

(2)   They extend to Greater Bombay

II.   Definitions: - In these by-laws, unless there be anything repugnant in thesubject or context.

(a)   "The Act" means the Bombay Nursing Homes Registration Act, 1949

(b)   "Corporation" means the Municipal Corporation of Greater Bombayconstituted under the Bombay Municipal Corporation Act, 1988 (here in after referred to as "The Municipal Act"

(c)   "Infections disease" means any disease which a medical practitioneris required to notify to the Executive Health Officer of the Corporation as under Section 421 of the Municipal Act or any other law for the time being inforce;

(d)   "Keeper of a nursing home" means a person who has been dulyregistered by the Corporation in respect of a Nursing home under section 5 of the Act and whose registration has not been cancelled under section 7 of the Act.

III.   Record of patients received into or of children born in the Nursing Home: -The keeper of a Nursing Home shall keep and maintain.

(a)   In the form appended to these by-laws a register of patients receivedinto the Nursing Home;

(b)   A correct alphabetical index of the names of the patients admitted tothe nursing home;

(c)   A daily record of health of every patient who may be suffering fromacute illness;

(d)   A daily record of health of every woman admitted to the nursing

(e)   home for delivery and of every child born to such woman in nursinghome; and

(f)   A daily and weekly record of health of other patients.

2.   The Keeper of nursing home shall keep and maintain a register special form,of maternal and infant deaths occurring in the nursing home, and submit monthly returns thereof to the Executive Health Officer.

3.   Where the register referred to in sub clause (1) relates to a

woman who has been admitted for delivery and where a child b orn to such woman is removed with the consent of the keeper of a nursing hope and of the parents or mother, to the care of a person other than its father, guardian or relative, the keeper of such nursing home shall, in addition to the particulars specified in clause (1) also specify in the register the name and address of such person and the dateon which and the consideration for which the child was so removed.

IV.   Notice of death occurring in Nursing Home: -

(1)   If any death occurs in a nursing home, the keeper of the nursing homeshall within 24 hours from the occurrence of the death given in writing the notice of such death to the Executive Health Officer of theCorporation or he Registrar of Births and Deaths for the District,appointed under section 442 of the Municipal Act, within whosejurisdiction the nursing home is situated.

(2)   The notice may be sent by pre-paid post or in any other effectivemanner

(a)   The notice shall contain the particulars required to be entered in aregister sheet under Section 451 of the Municipal Act.

(b)   Within twenty-four hours of the conclusion of the inquest, if any, heldon the death of any patient admitted into a nursing home, the keeperof such home shall forward a report to the Executive Health Officer ofthe Corporation or the Registrar of Births and Deaths for the Districtconcerned, containing the following particulars, namely: -

(c)   Date of inquest;

(d)   Cause of death as found by the authority by which the inquest washeld.

(e)   Penalty: - Any person who contravenes the provisions of any of thesebye- laws, shall, on conviction, be punished: -

(f)   With fine which may extend to fifty rupees, or

(g)   With fine which may extend to fifty rupees and in the case of acontinuing contravention with an additional fine which may extend to fifteen rupees for every day during which such contravention after conviction for the first such contravention, or

With fine Which may extend to fifteen rupees for every day duringwhich the contravention continues after the receipt of a notice fromthe Corporation by the person contravening the by-laws, requiringsuch person to discontinue such contravention.

To,

The Municipal Commissioner, Bombay

Urban Development & Public Health Department Sachivalaya, Bombay 400032 dated the 9ᵗʰ November 1976

BOMBAY NURSING HOMES REGISTRATION ACT, 1949

No. MNH-1173/30748-(349)-PH-10: - In exercise of the powers conferred by sub-section

(2) of section 4 and clause (b) of sub-section (2) of section 16 of the Bombay Nursing Homes Registration Act, 1949 (Bom. XV of 1949) and of all other powers enabling it in that behalf; the Government of Maharashtra hereby makes the following rules, further to amend the Maharashtra Nursing / Homes Registration Rules 1973, the same having been previously published as required by sub-section (3) of the said section 16 namely:

RULES

1.   These   rules   may   be called   the   Maharashtra   Nursing Homes Registration(Amendment) Rules, 1976

2.   In rule 7 of the Maharashtra Nursing Homes Registration Rule 1973: -

(a)   In sub-rule (1)

(i)   In clause (a) for the figures "20" the figures "50"shall be substituted;

(ii)   In clause (b) for the figures "50" the figures "100" shall be substituted.

(b)   In sub-rule (2) for the words "one half of" the words "equal to" shall besubstituted

By order and in the name of the Governor of Maharashtra,

Sd/-(S.V.Abhyankar)

Desk Officer

(These rules are amended by this notification for the first time).

. . . .

No. HO/39039/R-I of 30.11.76

Copy forwarded to A.H.O. I to IV, M.Os. (H) & Sr.S.Is. A to T wards forinformation attention and necessary action. Revised fees should be effective from 1.4.1977 and therefore applications received from Jan. 77 renewal should accompany the revised fees.

Sd/-

Sd/-

D.E.H.O.

      H.O.

No. HO/45026/RI of

Copy recalculated to A.H.O. I to IV, M.OS. (H) & Sr. S.Is. A to T wards for information,attention and necessary action please.

PROCEDURE FOR GRANT OF CERTIFICATE OF REGI STRATION FOR NURSING HOME

LEGAL PROVISION

The nursing homes in Greater Bombay are controlled under the provision of the Bombay Nursing Home Registration Act, 1949, the Bombay Nursing Homes Registration Rules, 1973 and the Bombay Municipal Corporation Nursing Homes Registration Bylaws, 1954. Section 3 to 5 and 7 and 8 of the Act and rules 4 to 11 deal with registration of nursing homes. Section 3 of the Act lays down that no person shall carry on a nursing home unless he has been duly registered in respect of such nursing home. Section 6 of the Act prescribed penalty with fine to the extent of Rs. 500/- for non- registration and in the case of second or subsequent offence with imprisonment to the extent of 3 months or with fine to the extent of Rs. 500/- or with both. Section 12 of the Act prescribes penalty for contravention of any other provisions of the Act or anyprovisions of the rules.

The Bombay Municipal Corporation Nursing Homes Registration Bylaws, 1954 govern nursing homes in regard to the records to be kept of the patients received into nursing homes or children born therein, etc. The Bylaws also provide for penalty for the breach of their provisions.

The terms "Maternity Home" and "Nursing Home" have been defined undersection 2 of the Act as under: -

"Maternity Home" means any premises used or intended to be used, for the reception of pregnant women or of women in or immediately after childbirth. "Nursing Home" means any premises used or intended to be used, for the reception of persons suffering from any sickness, injury or infirmity and the providing of treatment and nursing for them, and includes a maternity home, and the expression to carry on a "nursing home" means to receive persons in a nursing home for any of the aforesaid purposes and to provide treatment or nursing h/ for them.

The Municipal Corporation of Greater Bombay is the 'Local

Supervising authority' as per the definition of the term given in the Act and is responsible for the enforcement of the legal provisions within its jurisdiction. The Corporation has, by its Resolution No. 596 dated 13.8.19.64 authorised the Municipal Commissioner, Deputy Municipal Commissioner, Executive Health Officer, Deputy Municipal Commissioner, Executive Health Officer, Deputy Executive Health Officers, Medical Assistant in charge Sections and Sanitary Inspectors to execute the provisions of the Bombay Nursing Homes Registration Act, 1949, and Rules and by-laws framed there under in Greater Bombay.

Any person carrying on or intending to carry on a nursing home has to apply inthe prescribed from (Form 'B') to the Medical Officer of Health of the ward concerned. The from of application is available on payment of rupee one from the office of the Medical Officer of Health a specimen form of the application is in the rules.

On receipt of the application, the premises where the nursing home is carried onor is intended to be carried on is inspected and a report about its suitability for registration is submitted to the higher authority The suitability is determined n the following considerations (Section 5):

1. Fitness of the applicant or his agent to carry on the nursing home. Management under qualified medical practitioner or qualified nurse andresident in the home.

Proper portion of qualified nurses among sons superintending or nursing the patientsin the home. (Please see Sec. 5(1) (a) & item 14(b) of the application form).

4.   If a maternity home is a qualified nurse on its staff

5.   Fitness of the premises in regard to situation, construction, accommodation,staffing or equipment

6.   Use of the premises for any improper r undesirable purposes.

ISSUE OF CERTIFICATE OF REGISTRATION

If the premises are found suitable, the applicant is informed in writing to pay the necessary fees for registration in the office of the Medical

Officer of Health.

On receipt of the fees for registration, the application is registered in the office of the M.O.H. in a register in Form 'A' as required under Rule 3 of the Rules and a certificate of registration duly signed is issued to the applicant. A specimen form of the certificate of Registration is in the rules.

PERIOD OF VALIDITY OF THE CERTIFICATE

A certificate of registration issued is valid until the 31st day of March nextfollowing the date on which it was issued.

The certificate must be displayed in a conspicuous place in the nursing home. (Please see Sec. 5(3)).

RENEWAL OF REGISTRATION

An application for renewal is to be January accompanied by the renewal feed. If the M.O.H. is satisfied that the application is in order, he will issue a fresh certificate of registration (Rule 6)

REFUSAL OR CANCELLATION OF REGISTRATION

The M.O.H. has the discretion to refuse to register an application for the reasons given in Section 5 of the Act and to cancel the registration as provided under Section of the Act.

However, the M.O.H. has to give to the applicant or/to the person registered, not less than one calendar month notice of his intention to make an order of refusal or cancellation giving reasons therefore. The notice should also contain intimation that the applicant or the person registered will be given in person or by a representative, an opportunity within one calendar.

LOST CERTIFICATE

If a certificate of registration is lost or destroyed, the holder may apply to the

M.O.H. for a fresh certificate. A certificate marked as "Duplicate" will be issued onpayment of Rs. 5/- (Rule 11).

Bylaws   :   Copy of Bylaws attached.

The following Act of the Bombay Legislature, having been assented to by the Governor on the 15th September 1959 is hereby published for general information

N. K. DRAVID Secretary to the Government of Bombay,

Legal Department

BOMBAY ACT No. XLII OF 1959

(First published, after having received the ascent of the Governor in the"Bombay Government Gazette" on the 19th September, 1959

An Act to extend the Bombay Nursing Homes Registration Act, 1949, tothe rest of the State of Bombay and to amend that Act

WHERAS the Bombay Nursing Homes Registration Act, 1949, extends only to the pro-Reorganisation State of Bombay, excluding the transferred territories;

AND WHEREAS no corresponding law exists in the rost of the State of Bombay; AND WHEREAS it is expedient that the Bombay Nursing Homes Registration

Act, 1949 be extended to the rest of the State of Bombay and in its application to the whole of the State be amended for certain purposes hereinafter appearing; It is hereby enacted in the Tenth Year of the Republic of India as follows: -

1.   This Act may be called the Bombay Nursing Homes Registration (Extensionand Amendment) Act, 1959

2.   The Bombay Nursing Homes Registration Act, 1949, is hereby extended tothat part of the State of Bombay to which, immediately before the commence month of this Act, it did not extend

3.   In the Bombay Nursing Homes Registration Act, 1949, in its application to thewhole of the State of Bombay (hereinafter refereed to as "the principal Act")in the long title, for the words "Province of Bombay" the words "State of Bombay" shall be substituted.

4.   In section 1 of the principal Act, for sub-section (2) the following shall besubstituted namely: -

(2) This section extends to the whole of the State of Bombay. The remainingprovisions of this Act extend to Greater Bombay, the Cities Poona and Ahmedabad as constituted under section 3 of the Bombay Provincial Municipal Corporations Act, 1949, the City of Nagpur as constituted under the City of Nagpur Corporation Act, 1918 and the Municipal Borough of Solapur. The State Government may by notification in the Official Gazette, direct that the said provisions shall extend to suchother areas as may be specified in the notification.

5.   In section 2 of the principal Act: -

(1)   After ciause (1), the following clause shall be inserted, namely: -

" (1-a) 'district' local board' in relation to any area other than a municipal area, means a district local board, district board, district Panchayat or Janapada Sabha or similar local authority established under any law for the time being in force relating to the constitution of such authorities and having jurisdiction over such area;"

(2)   After clause (3), the following clause shall be inserted, namely: -

"3-a) 'municipality' means a municipal corporation, municipality, municipal committee, town committee or similar local authority established under any law for the time, being in force relating tothe constitution of such authorities and 'municipal area' means the local area within the jurisdiction of a municipality;"

(3)   For clauses (7) and (8), the following clauses shall be substituted,namely: -

"(7) 'Qualified midwife' means a midwife registered or deemed to be registered under the Bombay Nurses, Midwives and HealthVisitors

Act, 1954 or any other corresponding law for the time being in force;

(2) "Local supervising authority" in the case of a municipal area means the municipalityestablished for such area, and in the case of any other area a district local boardestablished for the said area;

(3) "Maternity home" means any premises used, or intended to be used, for the reception of pregnant women or of women in or immediately after child birth;

1[(3a) "Municipality" means a Municipal Corporation, municipality, Municipal Committee, Town Committee or similar local authority established under any law for the time being in force relating to the constitution of such authorities and "Municipal Area" means the local area within the jurisdiction of a municipality;]

(4) "Nursing Home" means any premises used or intended to be used, for thereception of persons suffering from any sickness, injury or infirmity and the providing of treatment and nursing for them, and includes a maternity home; and the expression "To carry on a nursing home" means to receive persons in a nursing home for any of the aforesaid. Purposes and toprovide treatment or nursing for them;

5. "Prescribed" means prescribed by rules made under this Act;

6. "Qualified Medical Practitioner" means a medical practitioner registered under theBombay Medical Act 1912, or any other law for the time being in force;

2[7. "Qualified midwife" means a midwife registered or deemed to be registered underthe Bombay Nurses, Midwives and Health Visitors Act 1954 or any other corresponding law for the time being in force;

8. "Qualified Nurse" means a nurse registered or deemed to be registered under the Bombay Nurses, Midwives and Health Visitors Act 1954, or any other correspondinglaw for the time being in force;]

9. "Register" means to register under section 5 of this Act and the expressions "Registered" and "Registration" shall be construed accordingly;

10. "Rules" means rule made this Act

Prohibition to carry on nursing home without registration
3. No person shall carry on a nursing home unless he has duly registered in respect of such nursing home and the registration in respect thereof has not been cancelledunder section 7:

Provided that nothing in this section shall apply in the case of a nursing home 3[which is in existence in any area at the date of the coming into force of section 3 in that area] for aperiod of three months from such date or if an application for registration is

THESC THE
SCHEDULE

[*See* section 56

About the Author

Dr. Navin Kumar Gupta

Dr Navin Kumar Gupta is reputed and highly qualified Ophthalmologist based in Mumbai. He had extensive training in several reputed institutions in India and US. He is also an office bearer of the Bombay Nursing Home Owners Association.

Dr. Binoy Gupta, retired as Principal Chief Commissioner of Income Tax. He holds a Ph.D. in law and 7 PG Degrees and Diplomas. He has authored several books and written hundreds of articles. He is practicing in Consumer Commissions since 2006.